Name Leo
Date 9/5/2014

✫✫✫✫✫
100% ☺

■ Draw a line from top to bottom connecting the two

P9-DBX-888

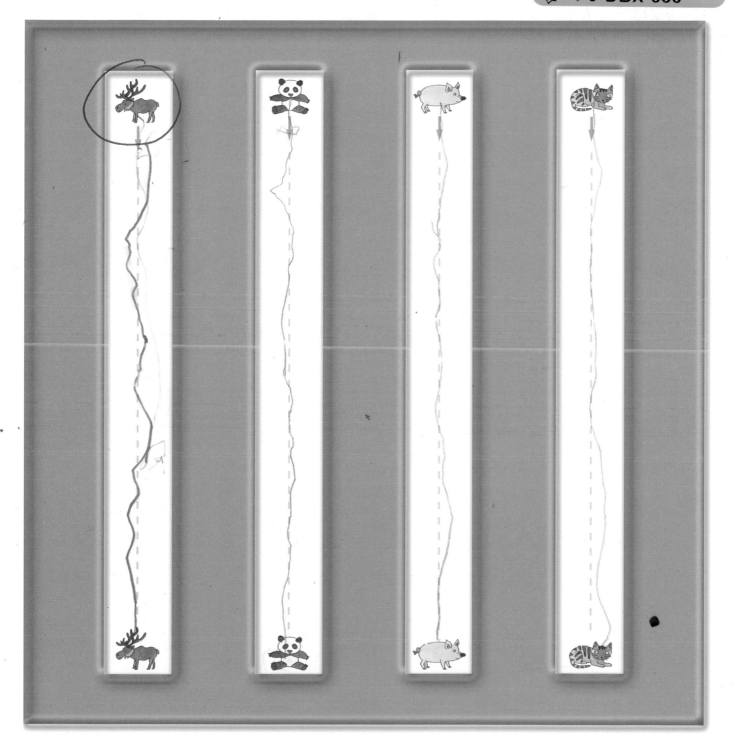

■Draw a line from top to bottom connecting the two pictures.

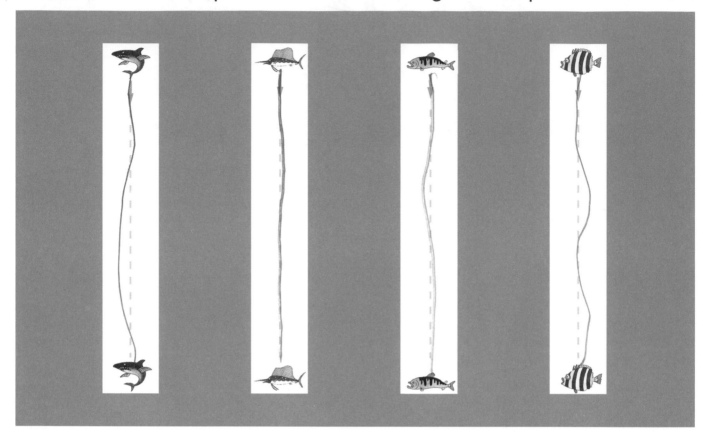

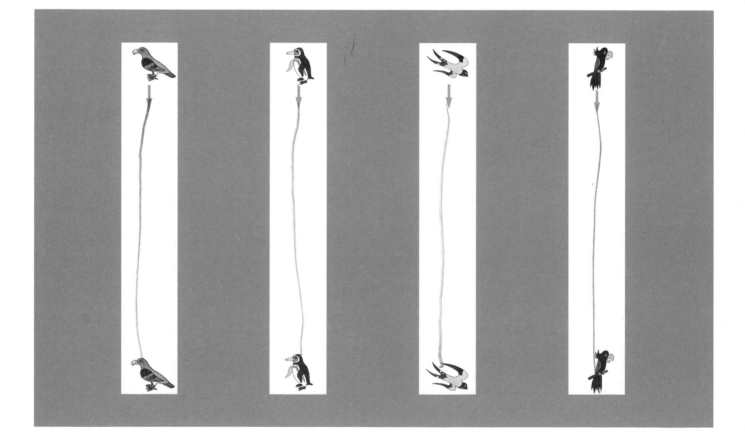

2 Drawing Horizontal Lines

Name

Date

■Draw a line from left to right connecting the two pictures.

■Draw a line from left to right connecting the two pictures.

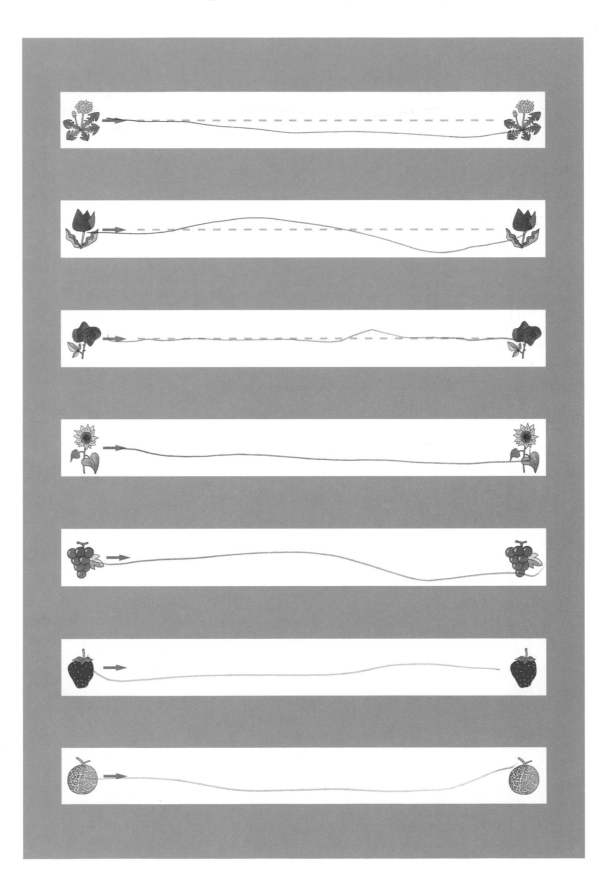

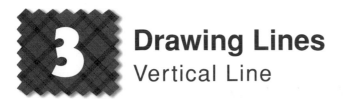
Name

Date

▪Draw a line from top to bottom connecting the two pictures.

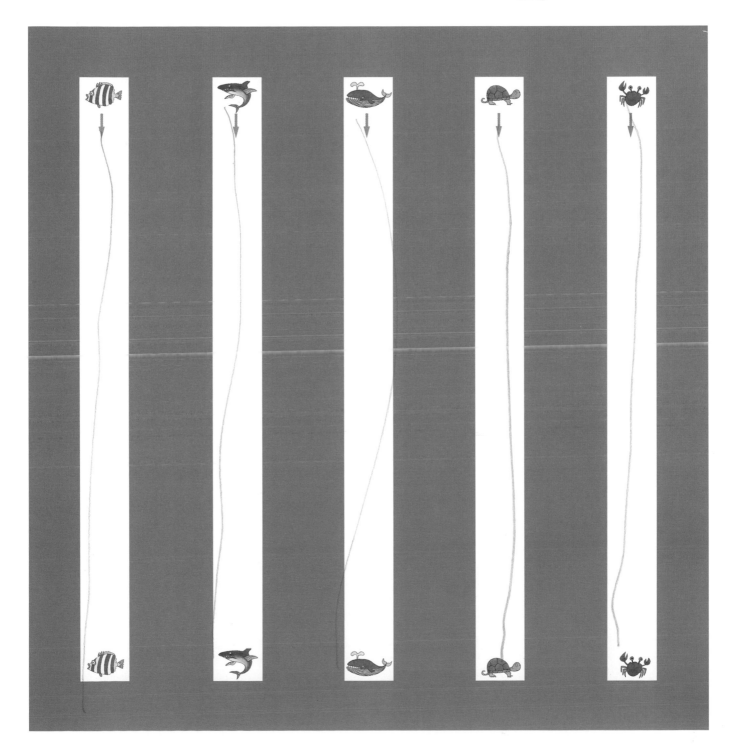

Horizontal Line

Anjali

■Draw a line from left to right connecting the two pictures.

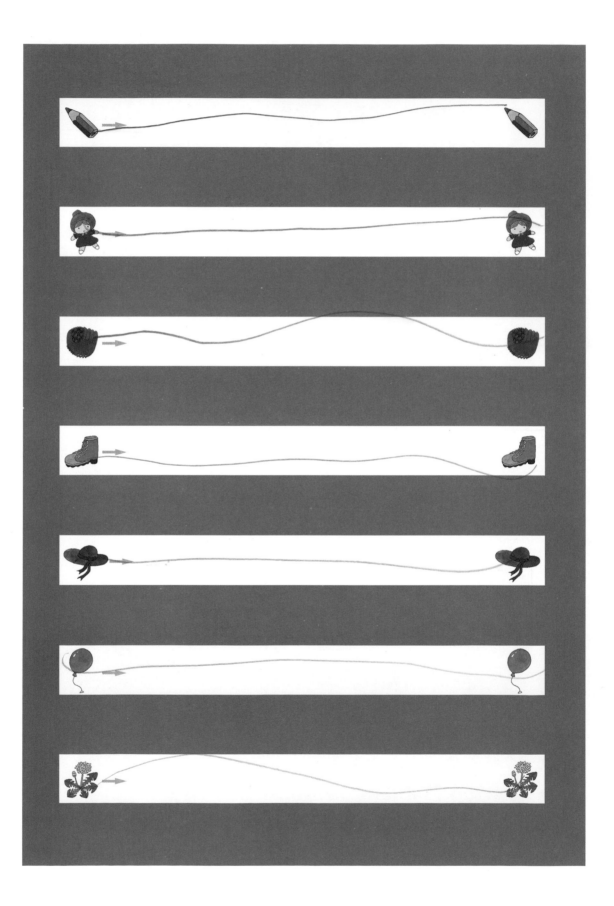

Tracing Letters
Writing L

Name _loooon mmnth_

Date _H n_

To parents
Before your child begins writing, please read the words on the page and ask your child to repeat the words after you. If your child can recognize the letters, it might be fun to have him or her tell you the name of each letter, and to have your child say the sound of the letter aloud while he or she traces it. If your child is still learning the alphabet, you should tell him or her the name of the letter and teach him or her its sound to say while tracing.

■ Draw a line from the dot (●) to the star (★).

L LION

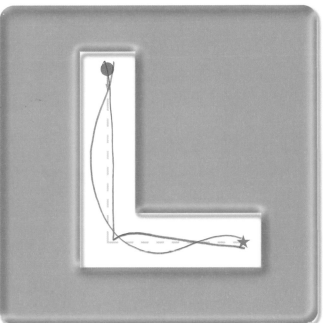

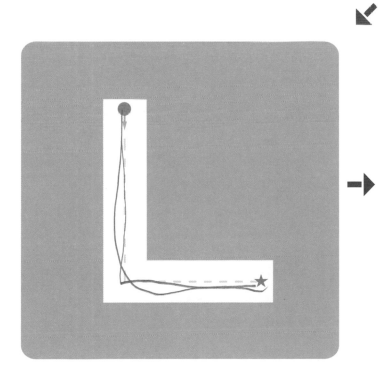

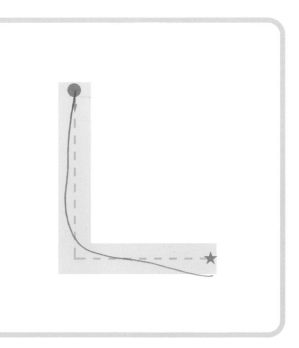

| A | B | C | D | E | F | G | H | I | J | K | L | M | N | O | P | Q | R | S | T | U | V | W | X | Y | Z |

Writing T

■Draw a line from the dot (●) to the star (★).
  Follow the order of the numbers.

T TOMATO

| A | B | C | D | E | F | G | H | I | J | K | L | M | N | O | P | Q | R | S | T | U | V | W | X | Y | Z |

Tracing Letters
Writing H

Name	
Date	

■Draw a line from the dot (●) to the star (★).
  Follow the order of the numbers.

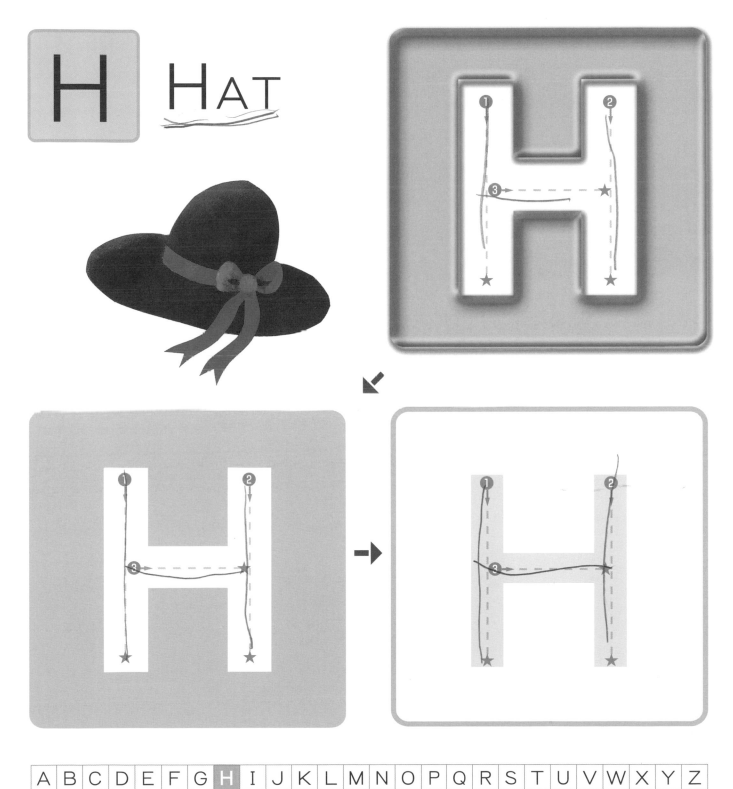

H   HAT

A B C D E F G H I J K L M N O P Q R S T U V W X Y Z

Writing L, T, and H

■Draw a line from the dot (●) to the star (★).
 Follow the order of the numbers.

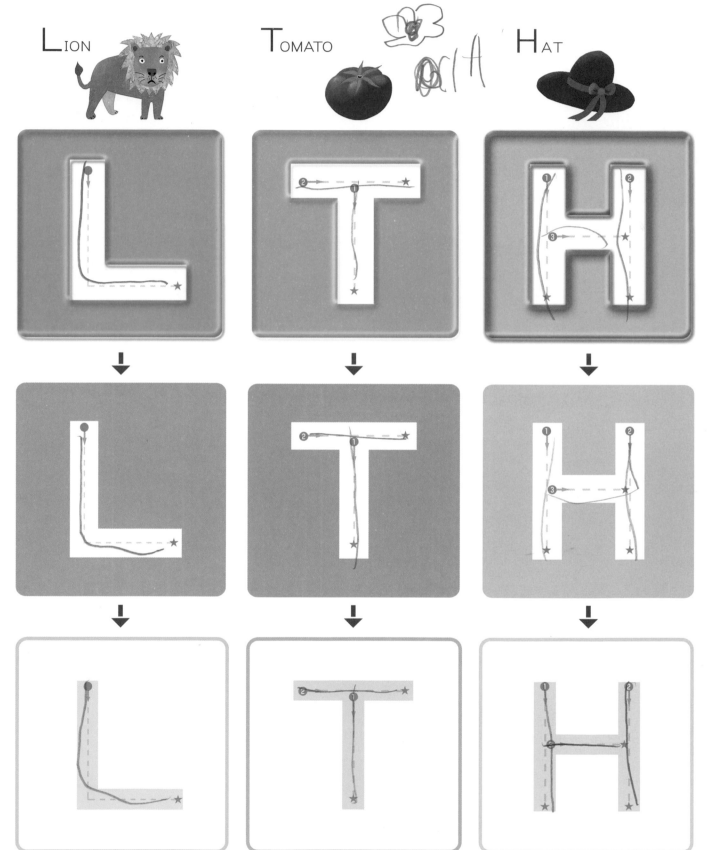

L_{ION}   T_{OMATO}   H_{AT}

6 Tracing Letters
Writing I

Name

Date

▪Draw a line from the dot (●) to the star (★).
 Follow the order of the numbers.

I INK

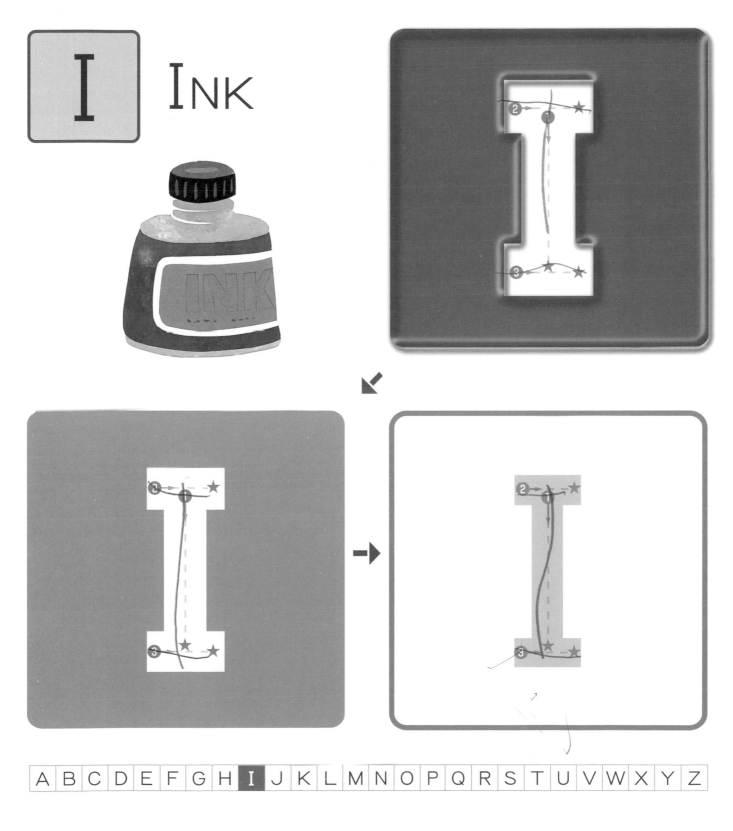

| A | B | C | D | E | F | G | H | **I** | J | K | L | M | N | O | P | Q | R | S | T | U | V | W | X | Y | Z |

Writing F

■Draw a line from the dot (●) to the star (★).
  Follow the order of the numbers.

F Fox

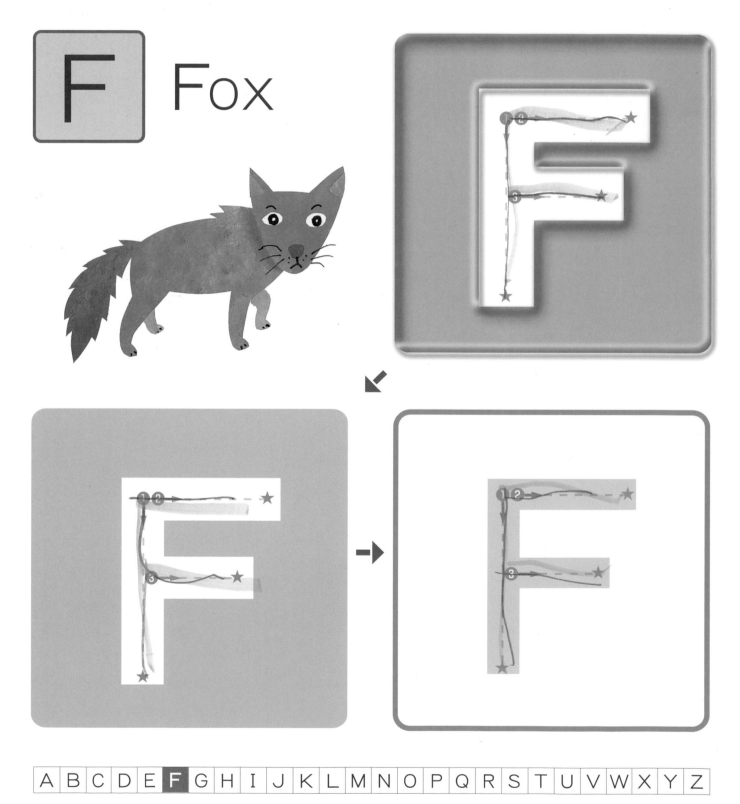

| A | B | C | D | E | **F** | G | H | I | J | K | L | M | N | O | P | Q | R | S | T | U | V | W | X | Y | Z |

Tracing Letters
Writing E

Name	
Date	

■ Draw a line from the dot (●) to the star (★).
Follow the order of the numbers.

E EGG

A B C D **E** F G H I J K L M N O P Q R S T U V W X Y Z

Writing I, F, and E

▪Draw a line from the dot (●) to the star (★).
 Follow the order of the numbers.

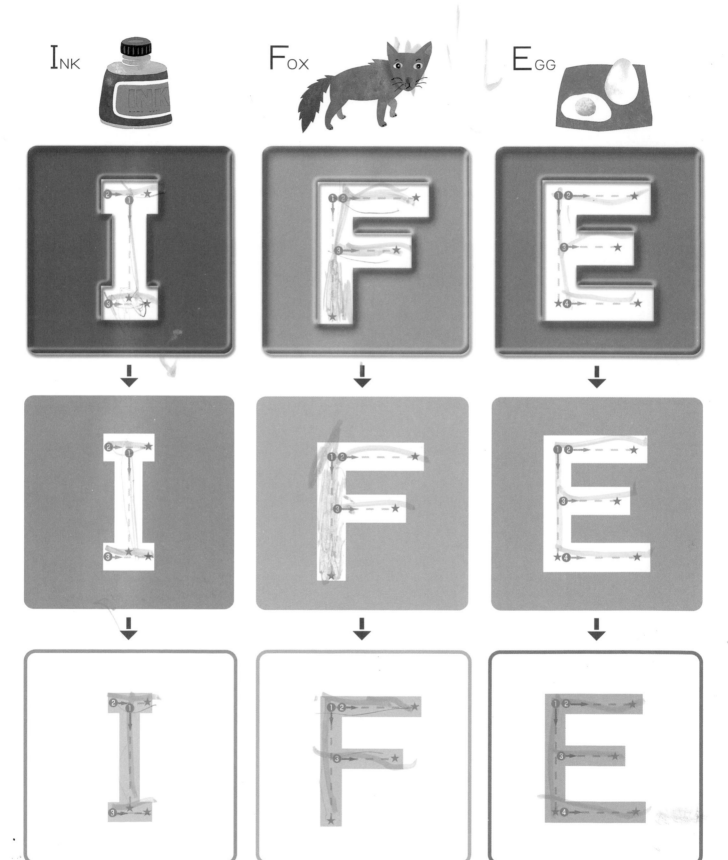

INK

FOX

EGG

Review
Writing L, T, and H

Name

Date

▪Draw a line from the dot (●) to the star (★).
Follow the order of the numbers.

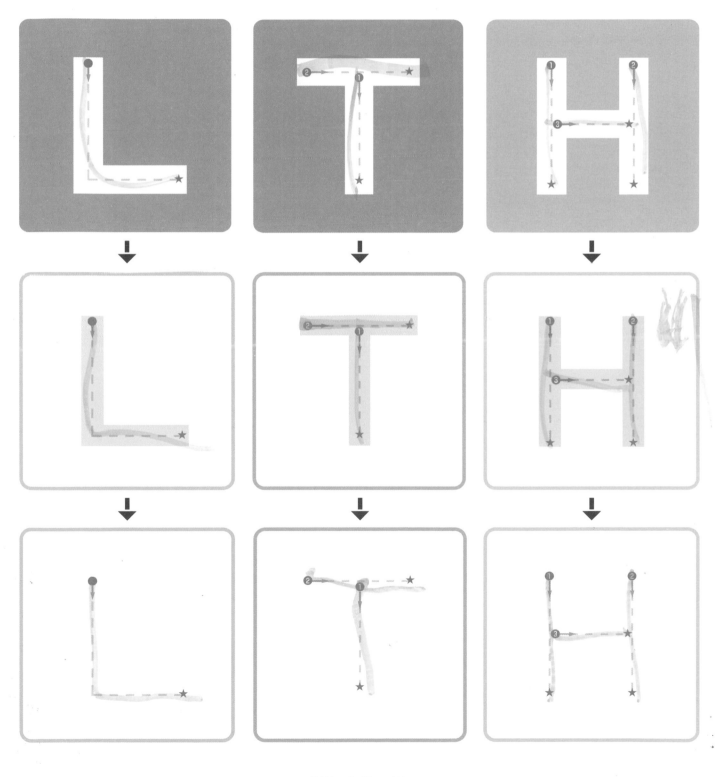

Writing I, F, and E

■Draw a line from the dot (●) to the star (★).
  Follow the order of the numbers.

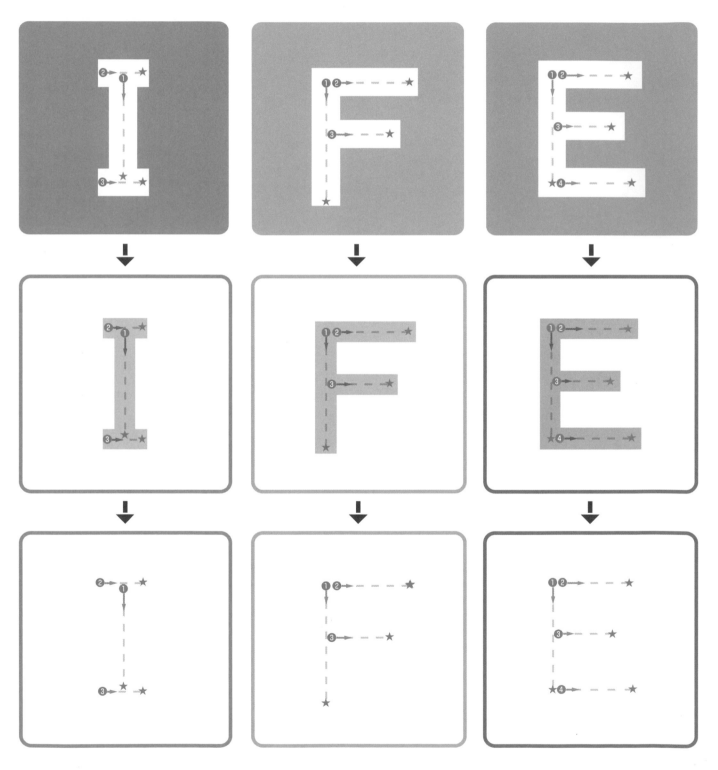

Drawing
Right Diagonal Lines

Name

Date

■Draw a line connecting each pair of pictures.

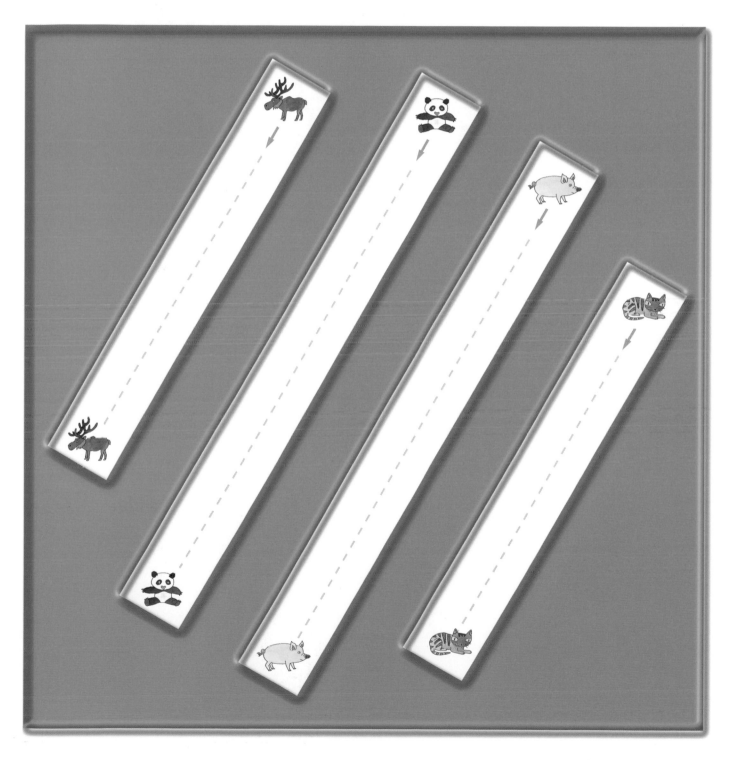

■Draw a line connecting each pair of pictures.

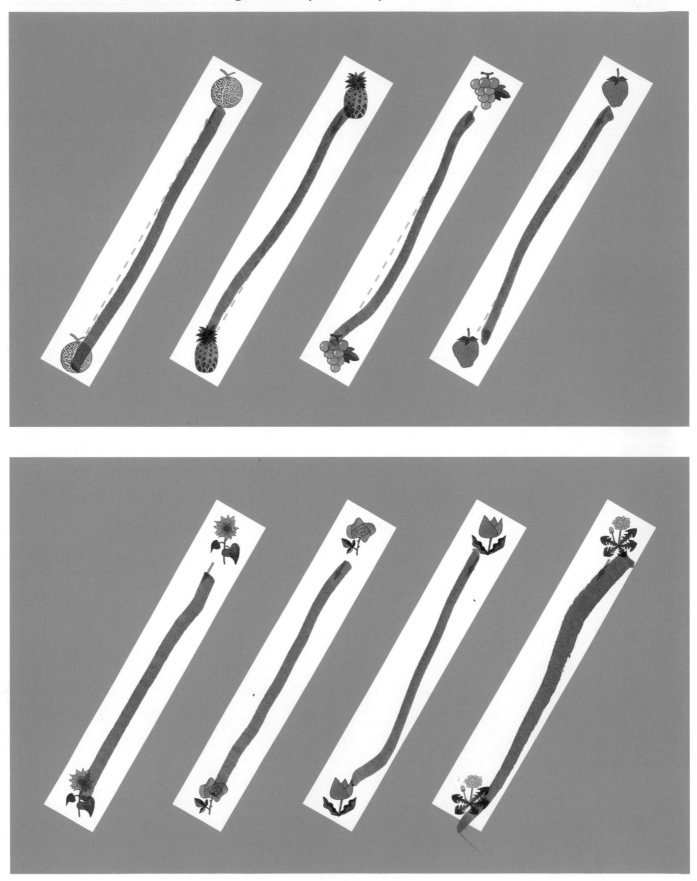

10 Drawing
Left Diagonal Lines

Name
Date

■Draw a line connecting each pair of pictures.

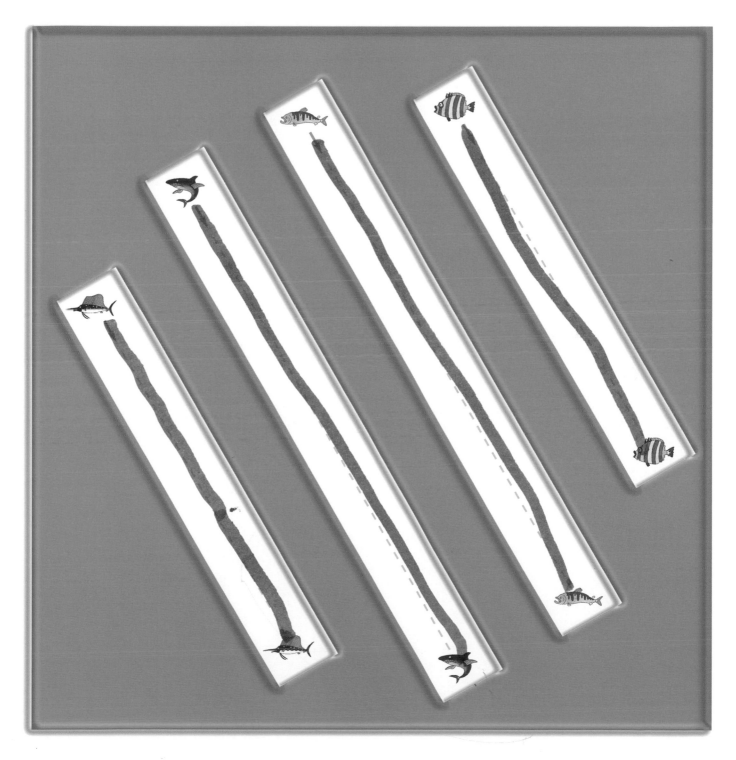

■Draw a line connecting each pair of pictures.

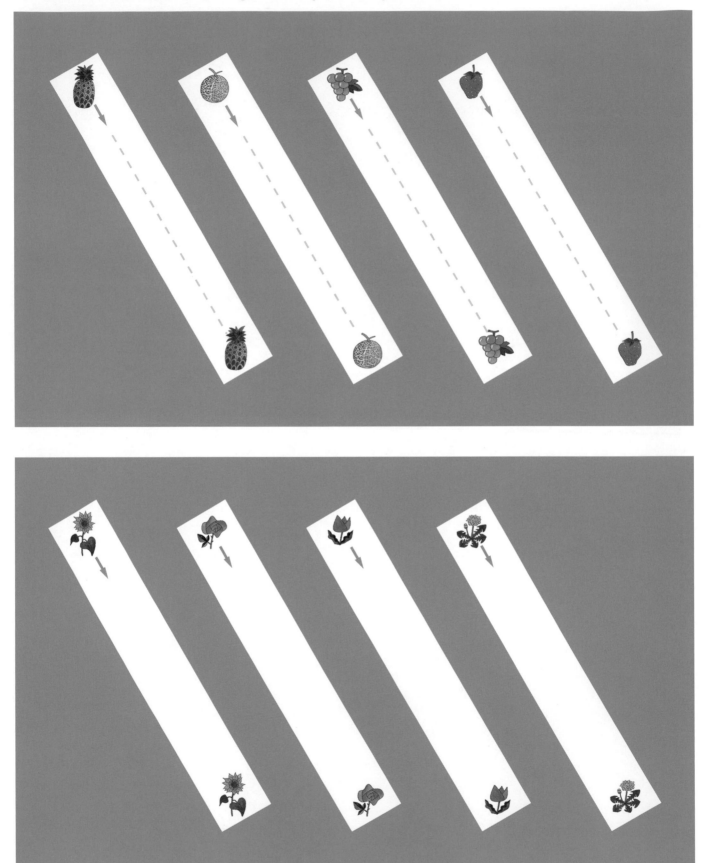

Drawing Lines
Right Diagonal Line

▪Draw a line connecting each pair of pictures.

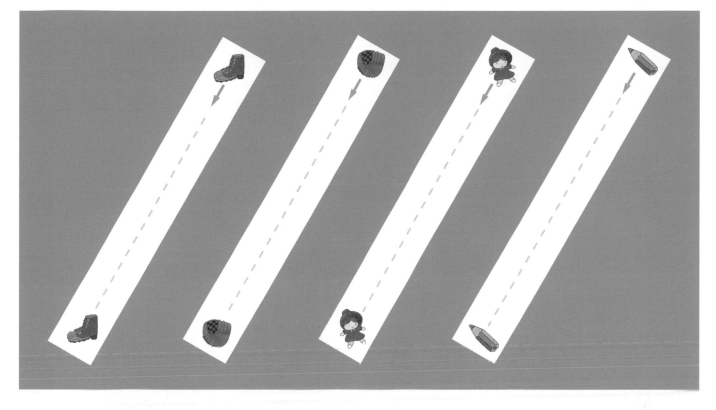

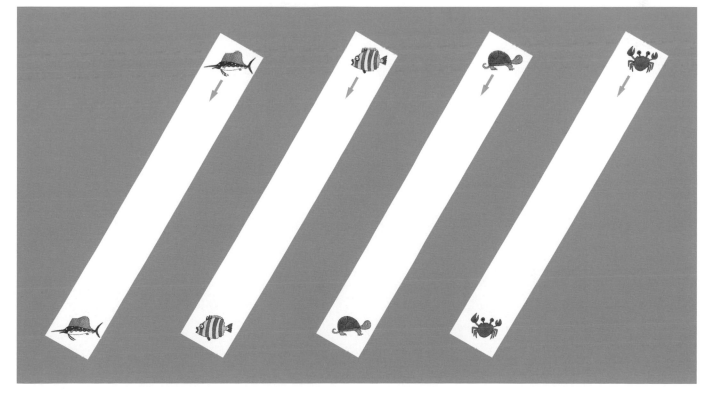

Left Diagonal Line

▪Draw a line connecting each pair of pictures.

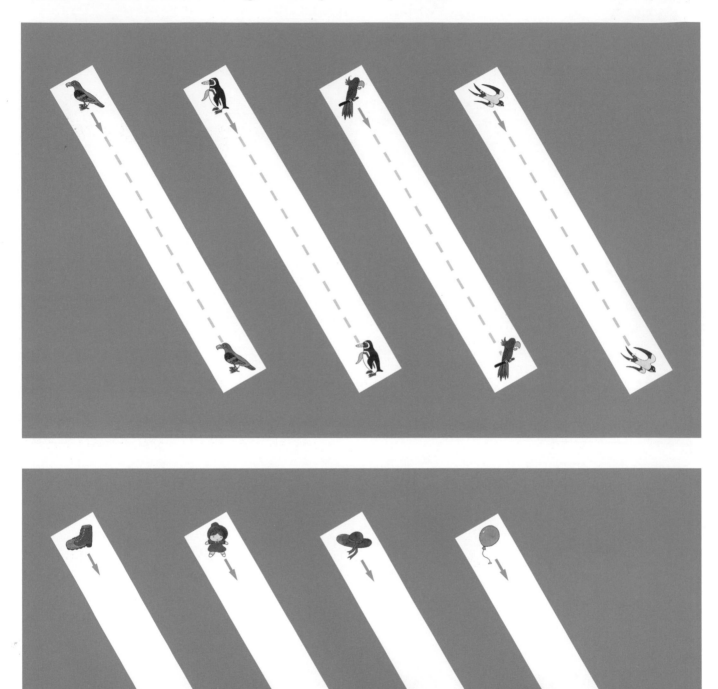

Tracing Letters
Writing X

Name	
Date	

■ Draw a line from the dot (●) to the star (★).
 Follow the order of the numbers.

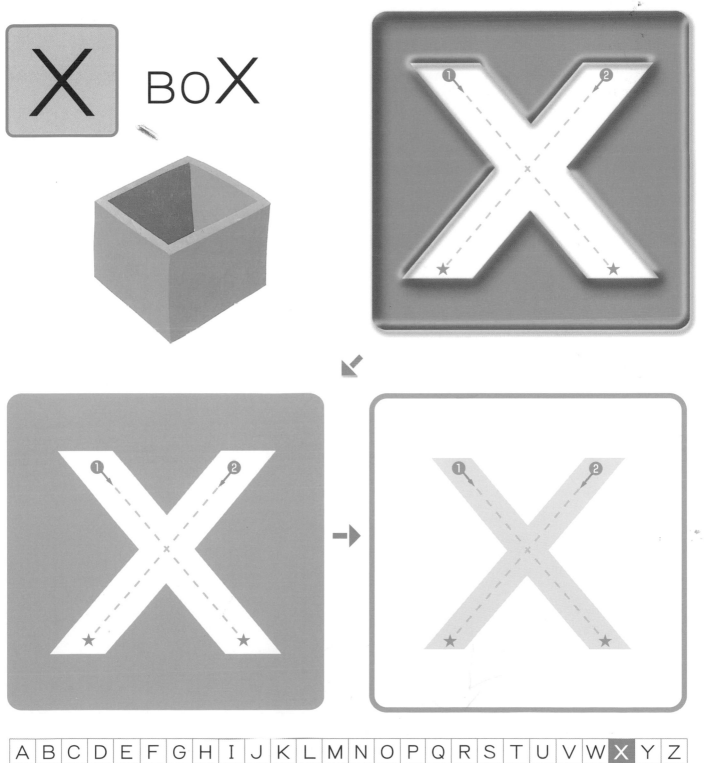

X BOX

A B C D E F G H I J K L M N O P Q R S T U V W X Y Z

Writing V

■Draw a line from the dot (●) to the star (★).

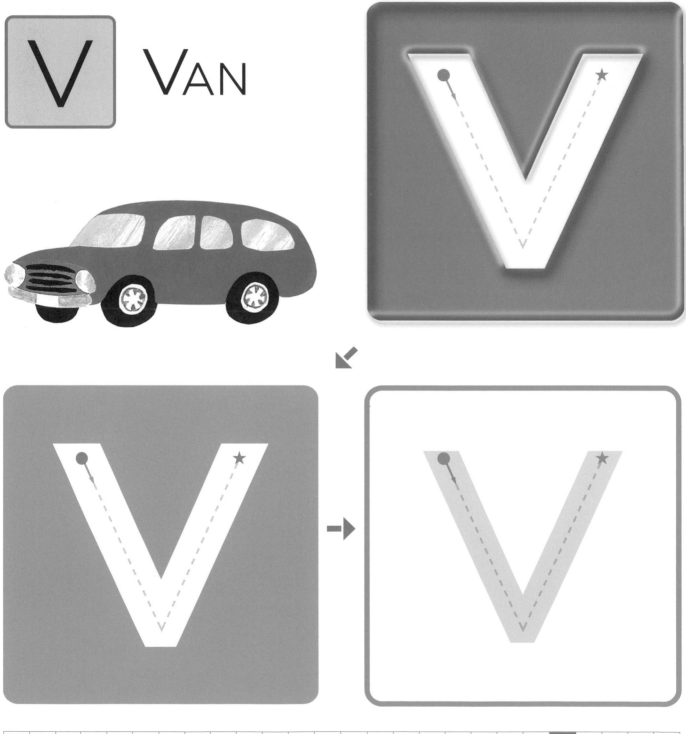

V VAN

| A | B | C | D | E | F | G | H | I | J | K | L | M | N | O | P | Q | R | S | T | U | V | W | X | Y | Z |

Tracing Letters
Writing Y

Name

Date

▪ Draw a line from the dot (●) to the star (★).
Follow the order of the numbers.

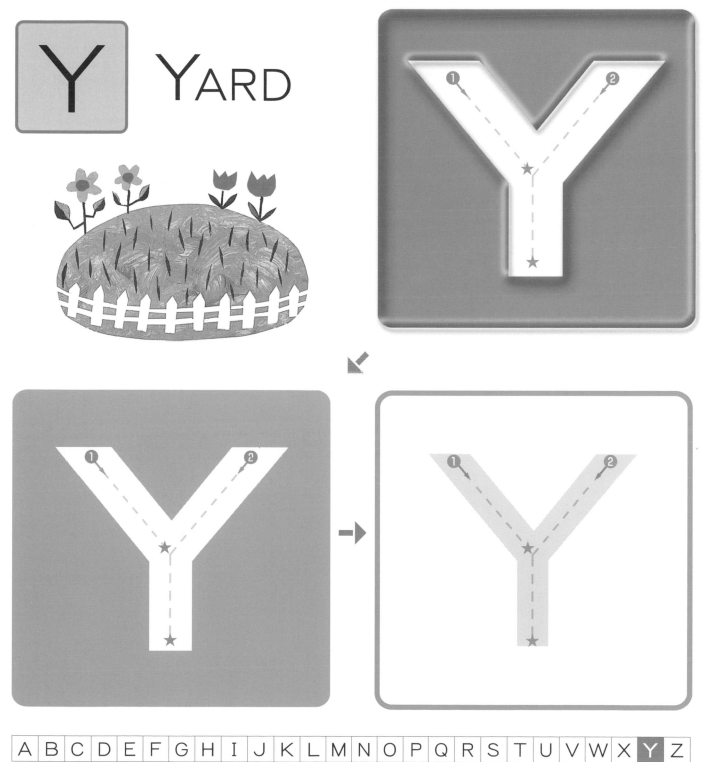

Y YARD

| A | B | C | D | E | F | G | H | I | J | K | L | M | N | O | P | Q | R | S | T | U | V | W | X | Y | Z |

Writing X, V, and Y

■Draw a line from the dot (●) to the star (★).
Follow the order of the numbers.

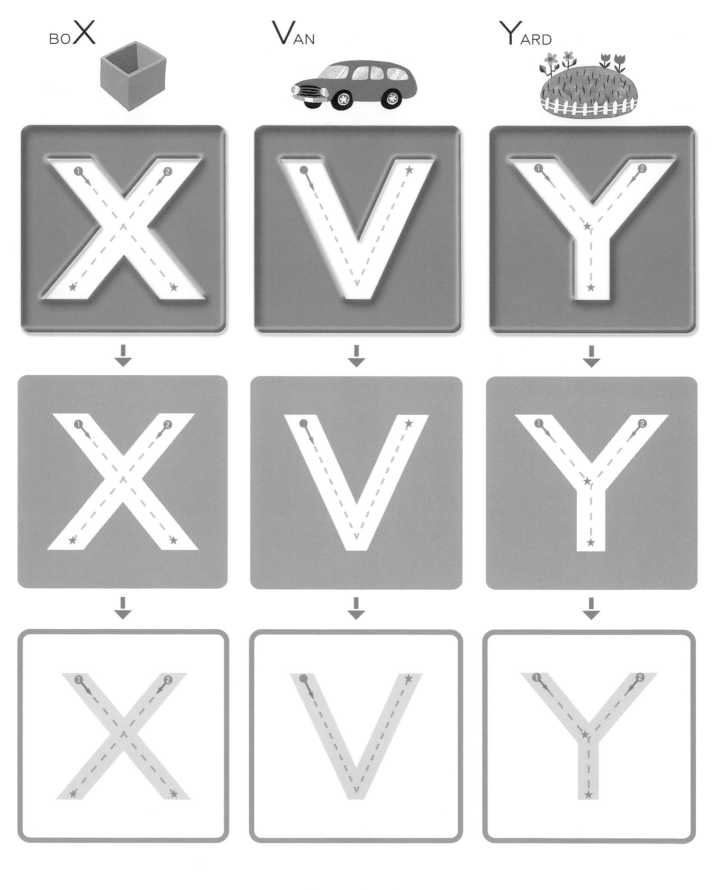

BOX VAN YARD

Tracing Letters
Writing N

■Draw a line from the dot (●) to the star (★).
Follow the order of the numbers.

N Nut

A B C D E F G H I J K L M N O P Q R S T U V W X Y Z

Writing Z

■Draw a line from the dot (●) to the star (★).

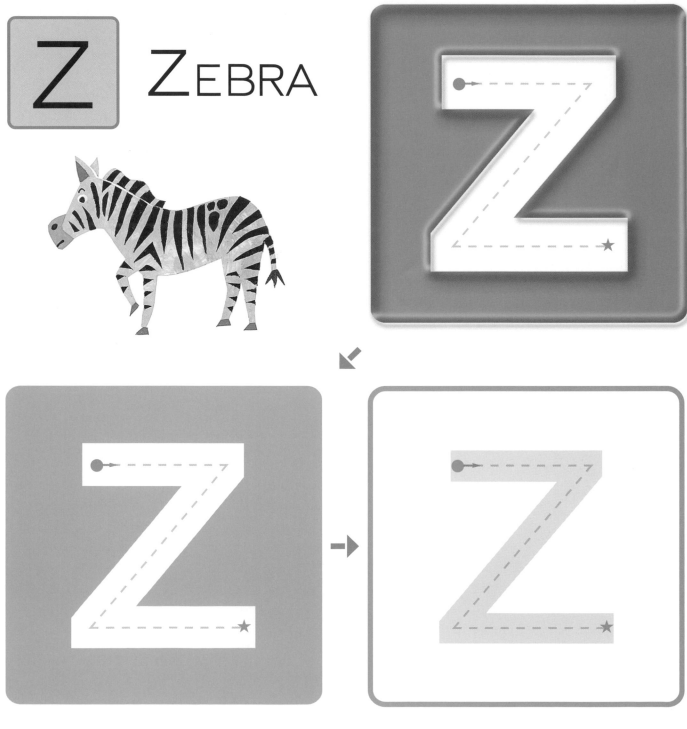

Z ZEBRA

| A | B | C | D | E | F | G | H | I | J | K | L | M | N | O | P | Q | R | S | T | U | V | W | X | Y | Z |

Tracing Letters
Writing A

Name	
Date	

■Draw a line from the dot (●) to the star (★).
　Follow the order of the numbers.

A ANT

A B C D E F G H I J K L M N O P Q R S T U V W X Y Z

Writing N, Z, and A

■Draw a line from the dot (●) to the star (★).
  Follow the order of the numbers.

Nᴜᴛ   Zᴇʙʀᴀ   Aɴᴛ

16 Tracing Letters
Writing K

Name

Date

■Draw a line from the dot (●) to the star (★).
Follow the order of the numbers.

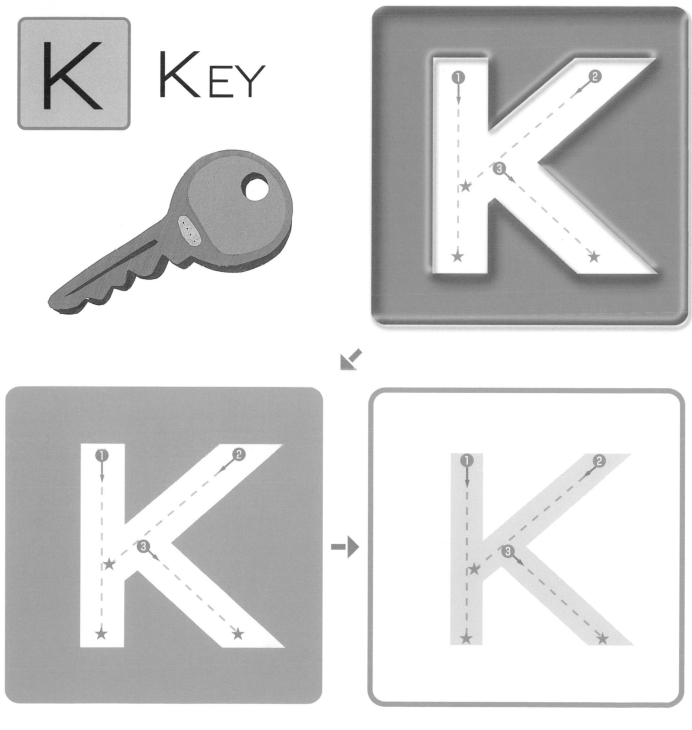

K KEY

A B C D E F G H I J K L M N O P Q R S T U V W X Y Z

Writing M

- Draw a line from the dot (●) to the star (★).
  Follow the order of the numbers.

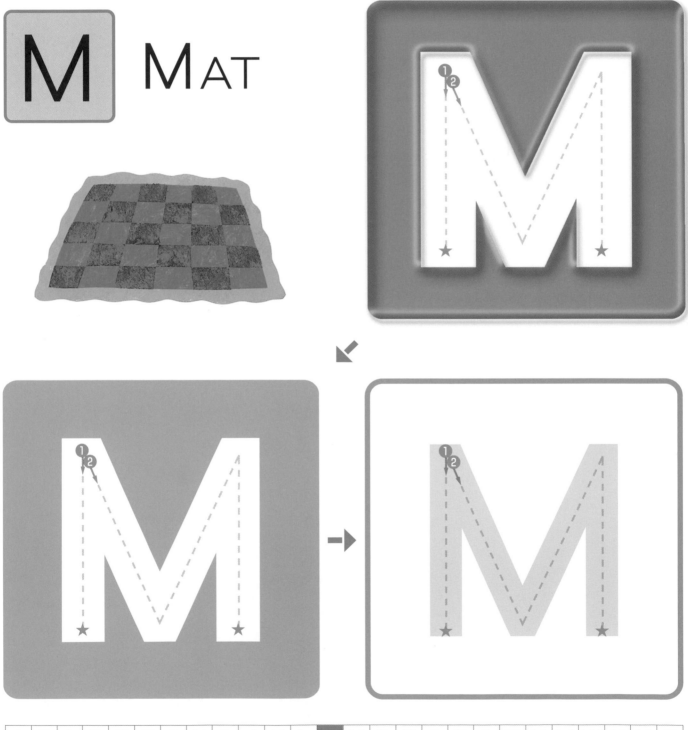

M MAT

| A | B | C | D | E | F | G | H | I | J | K | L | M | N | O | P | Q | R | S | T | U | V | W | X | Y | Z |

Tracing Letters
Writing W

Name

Date

■Draw a line from the dot (●) to the star (★).

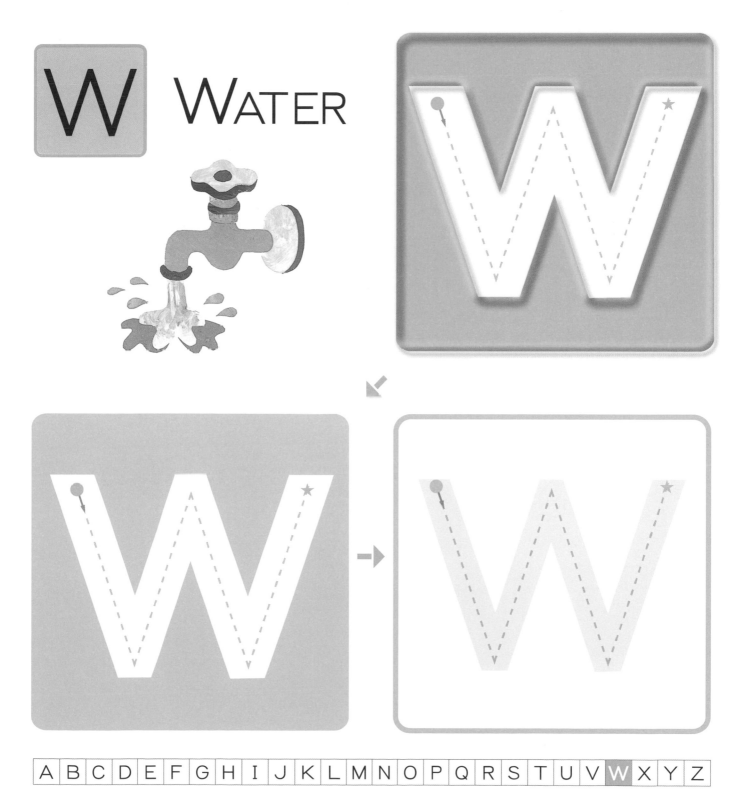

W WATER

| A | B | C | D | E | F | G | H | I | J | K | L | M | N | O | P | Q | R | S | T | U | V | W | X | Y | Z |

Writing K, M, and W

■ Draw a line from the dot (●) to the star (★).
Follow the order of the numbers.

K_{EY}   M_{AT}   W_{ATER}

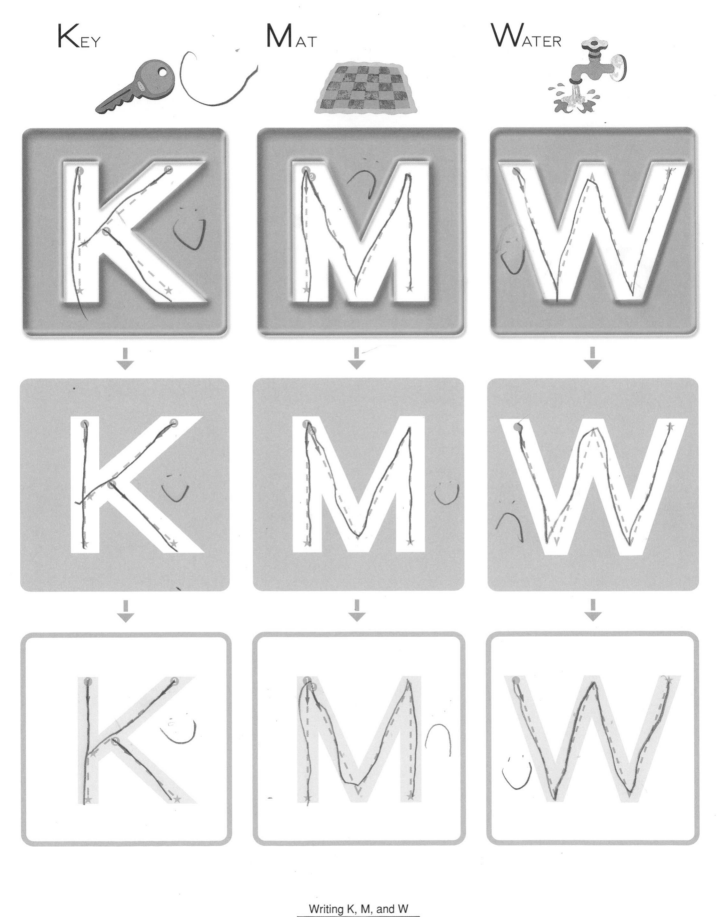

Review
Writing X, V, and Y

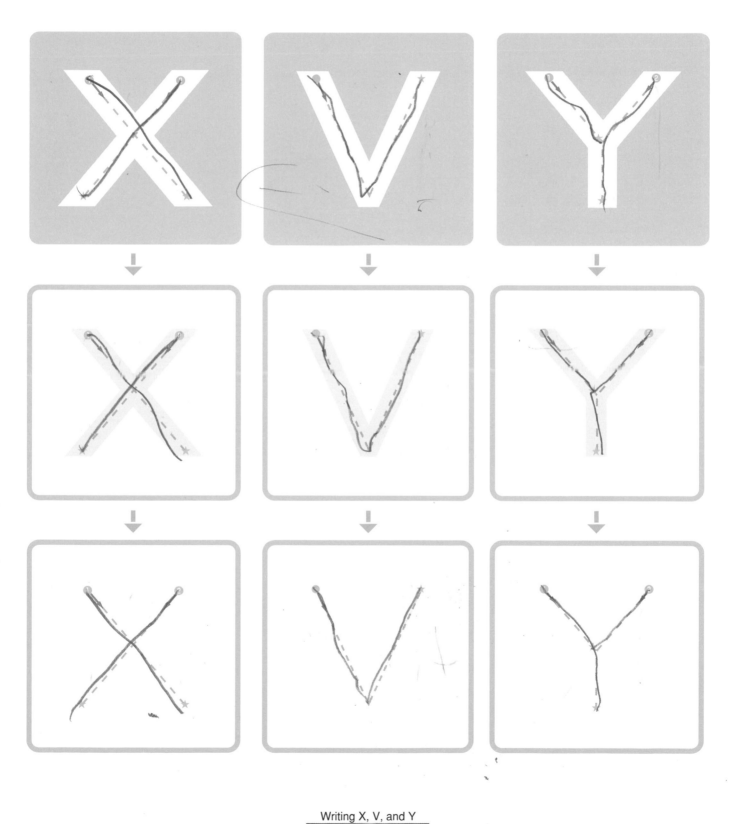

■Draw a line from the dot (●) to the star (★).
 Follow the order of the numbers.

Writing N, Z, and A

■Draw a line from the dot (●) to the star (★).
  Follow the order of the numbers.

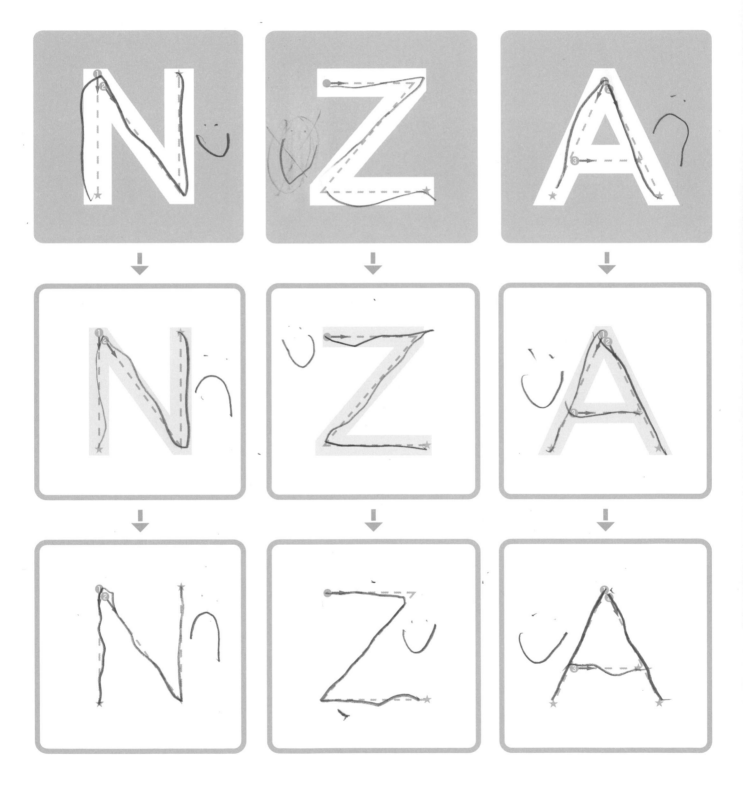

Review

Writing K, M, and W

■ Draw a line from the dot (●) to the star (★).
Follow the order of the numbers.

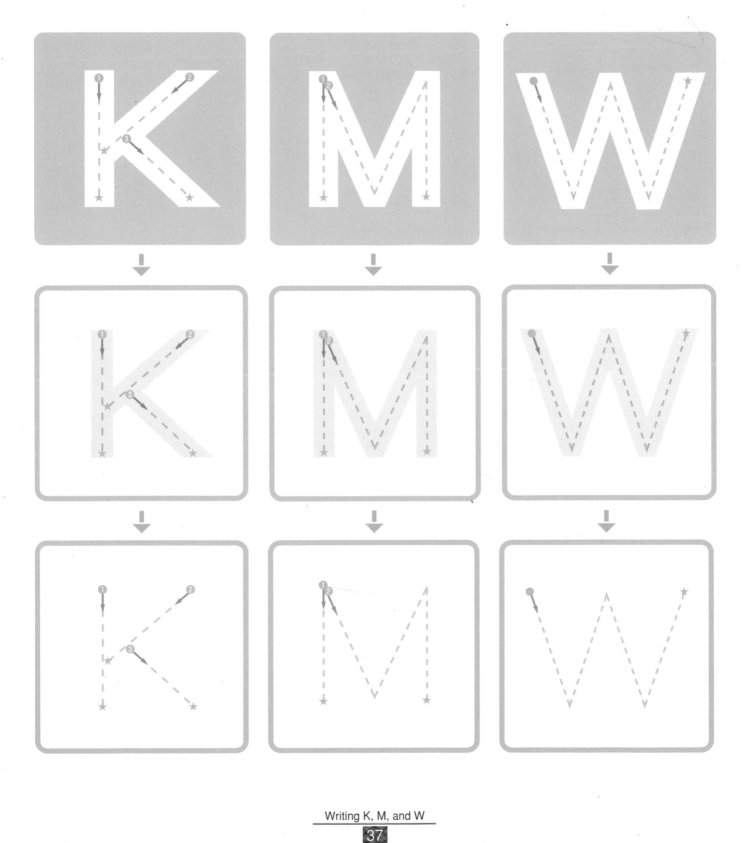

■Trace the letters below.

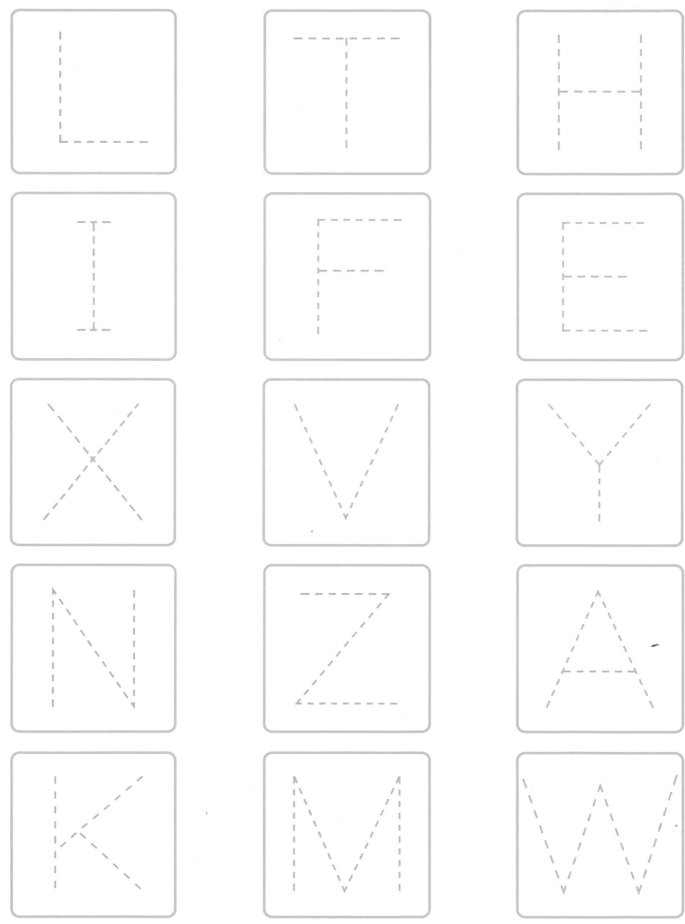

■Draw a line connecting each pair of pictures.

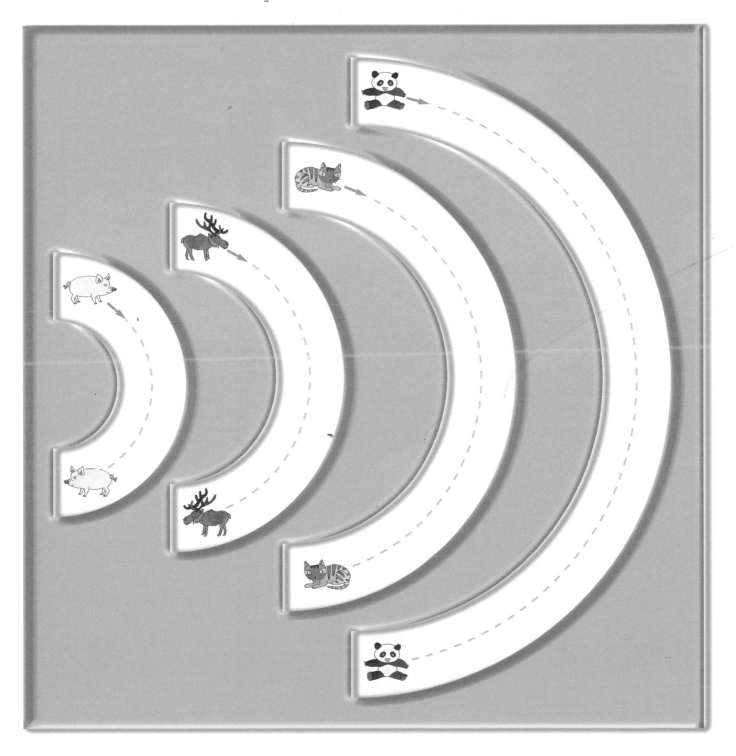

■Draw a line connecting each pair of pictures.

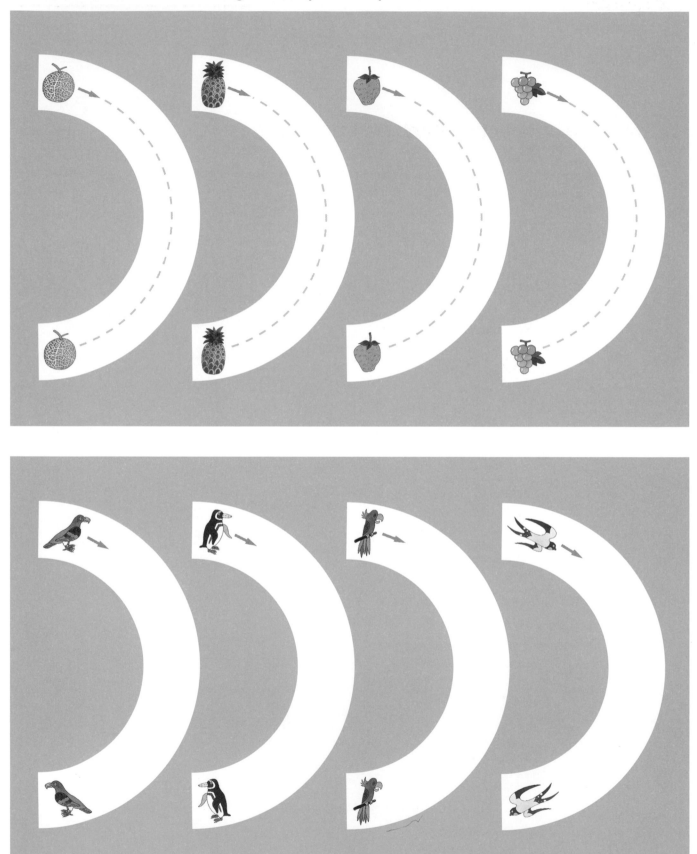

21 Drawing Left Curved Lines

■Draw a line connecting each pair of pictures.

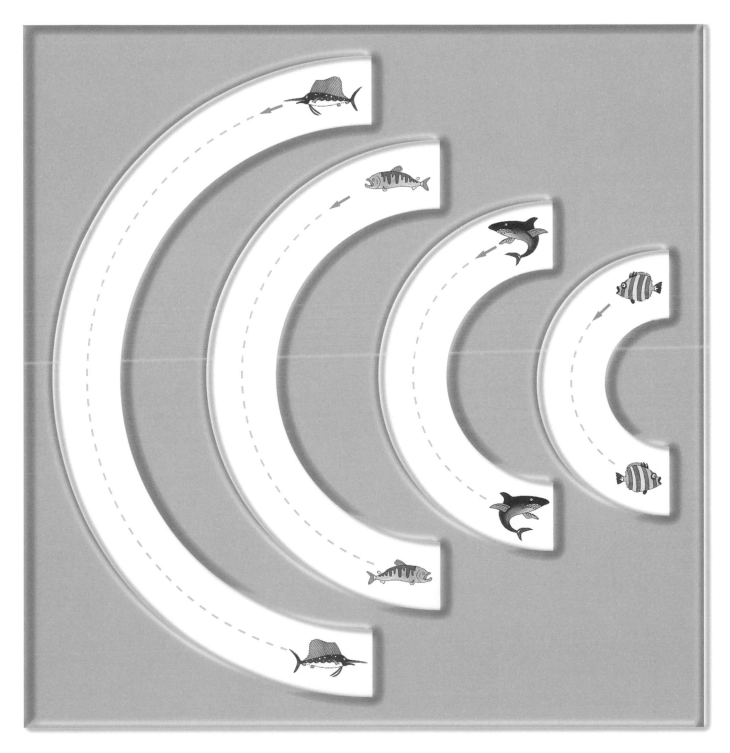

■Draw a line connecting each pair of pictures.

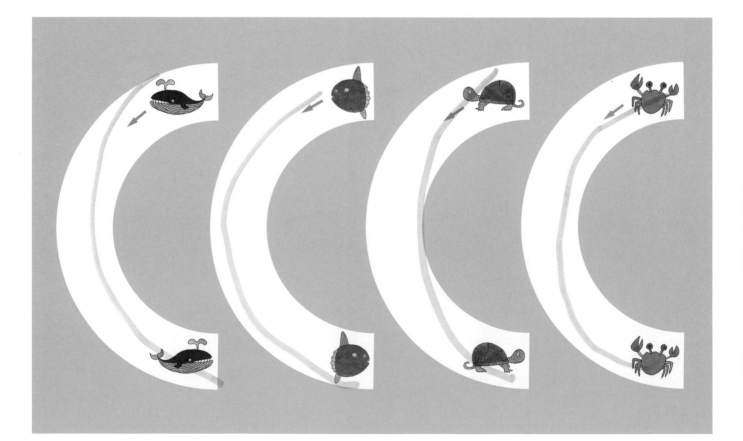

22 Drawing Lines
Right Curved Line

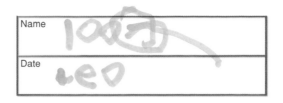

■Draw a line connecting each pair of pictures.

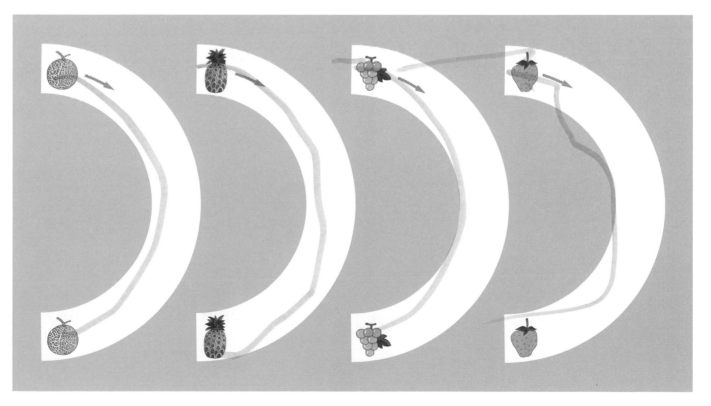

Left Curved Line

▪Draw a line connecting each pair of pictures.

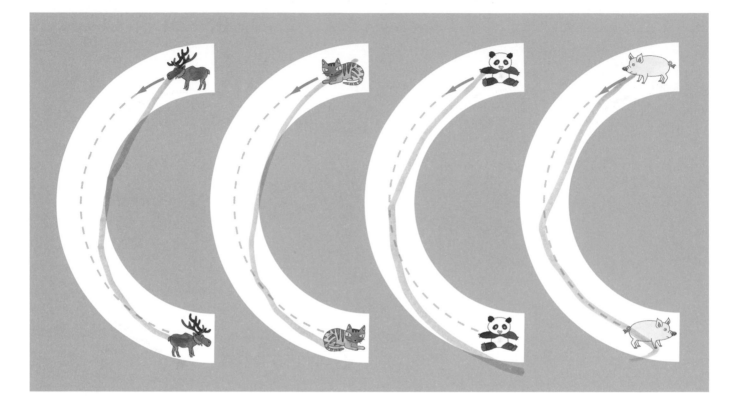

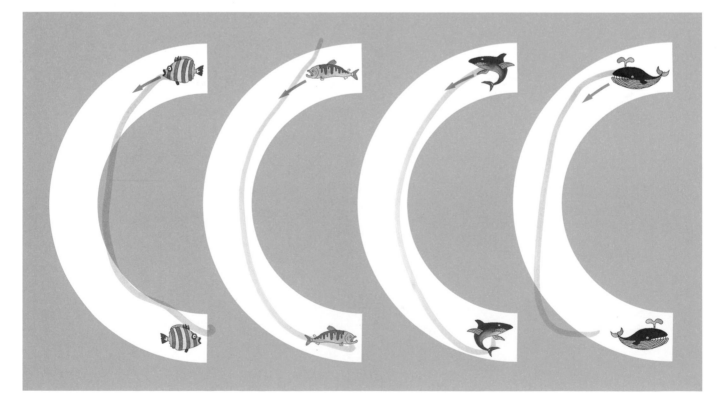

Tracing Letters
Writing D

■Draw a line from the dot (●) to the star (★).
Follow the order of the numbers.

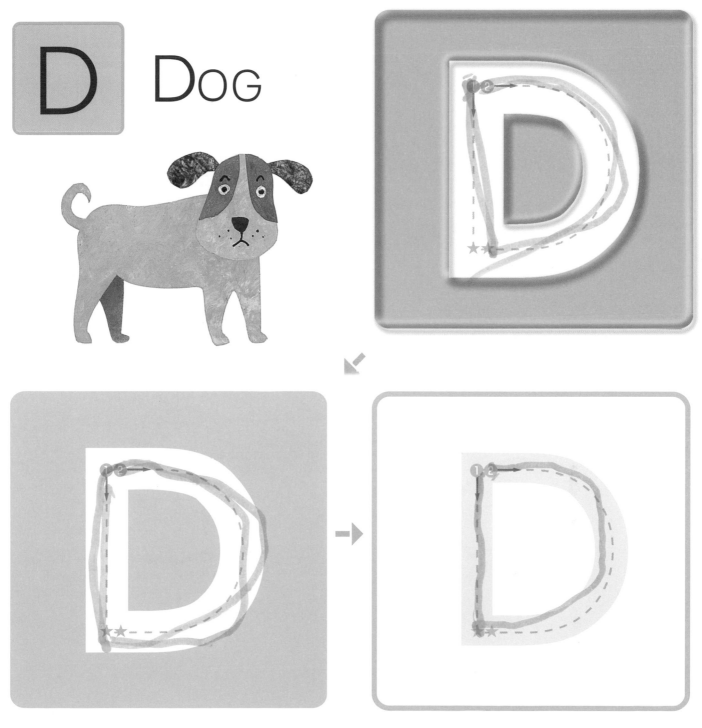

D Dog

A B C D E F G H I J K L M N O P Q R S T U V W X Y Z

Writing P

■Draw a line from the dot (●) to the star (★).
 Follow the order of the numbers.

P P<small>AN</small>

| A | B | C | D | E | F | G | H | I | J | K | L | M | N | O | P | Q | R | S | T | U | V | W | X | Y | Z |

Tracing Letters
Writing B

■Draw a line from the dot (●) to the star (★).
 Follow the order of the numbers.

B   BAG

| A | B | C | D | E | F | G | H | I | J | K | L | M | N | O | P | Q | R | S | T | U | V | W | X | Y | Z |

Writing D, P, and B

■Draw a line from the dot (●) to the star (★).
  Follow the order of the numbers.

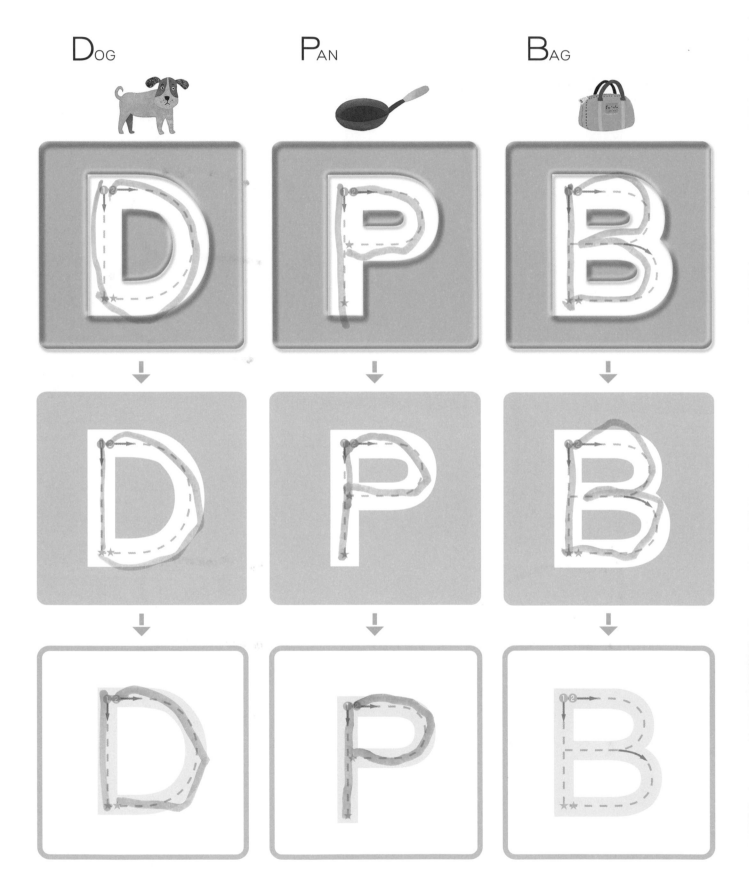

Dog

Pan

Bag

Name
Date

■Draw a line from the dot (●) to the star (★).
  Follow the order of the numbers.

R | RAT

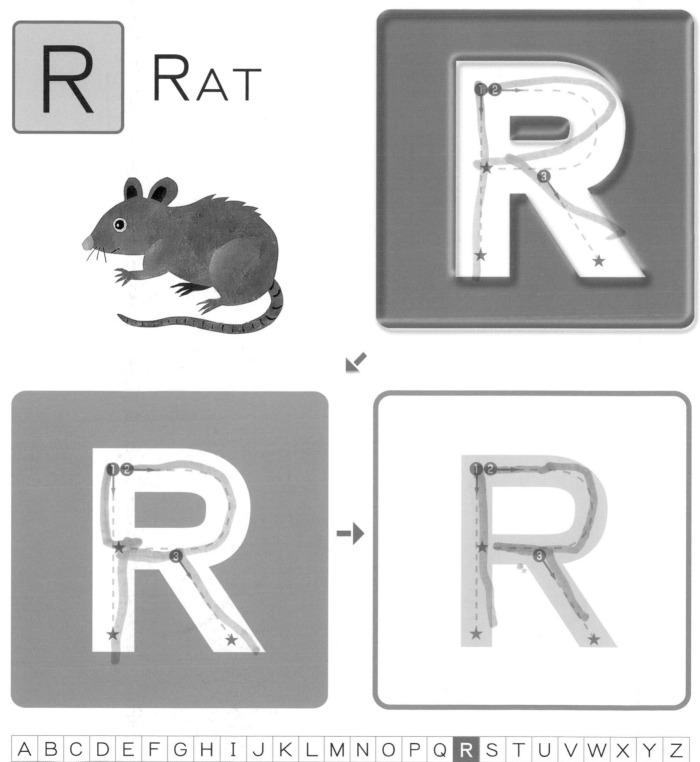

| A | B | C | D | E | F | G | H | I | J | K | L | M | N | O | P | Q | **R** | S | T | U | V | W | X | Y | Z |

Writing J

■Draw a line from the dot (●) to the star (★).

J JAM

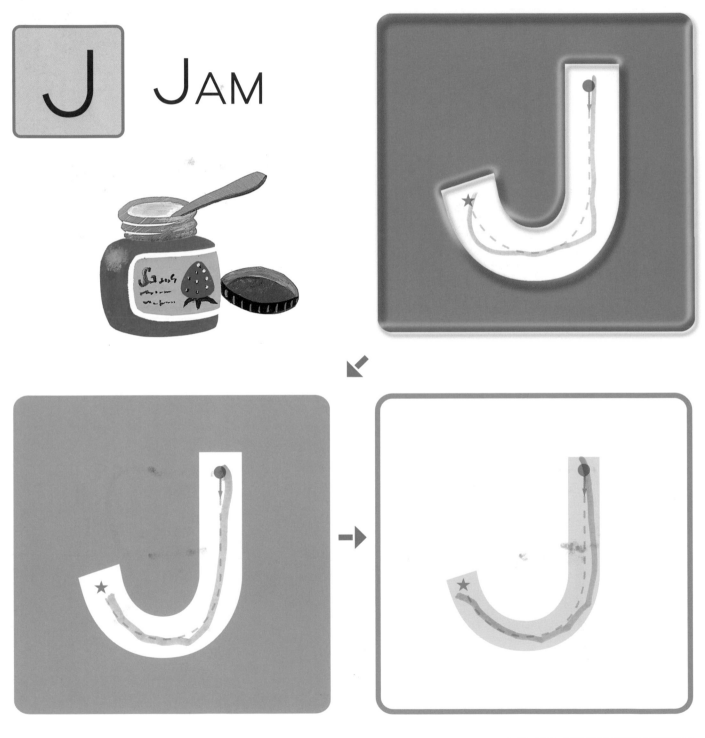

| A | B | C | D | E | F | G | H | I | J | K | L | M | N | O | P | Q | R | S | T | U | V | W | X | Y | Z |

Name	
Date	

■Draw a line from the dot (●) to the star (★).

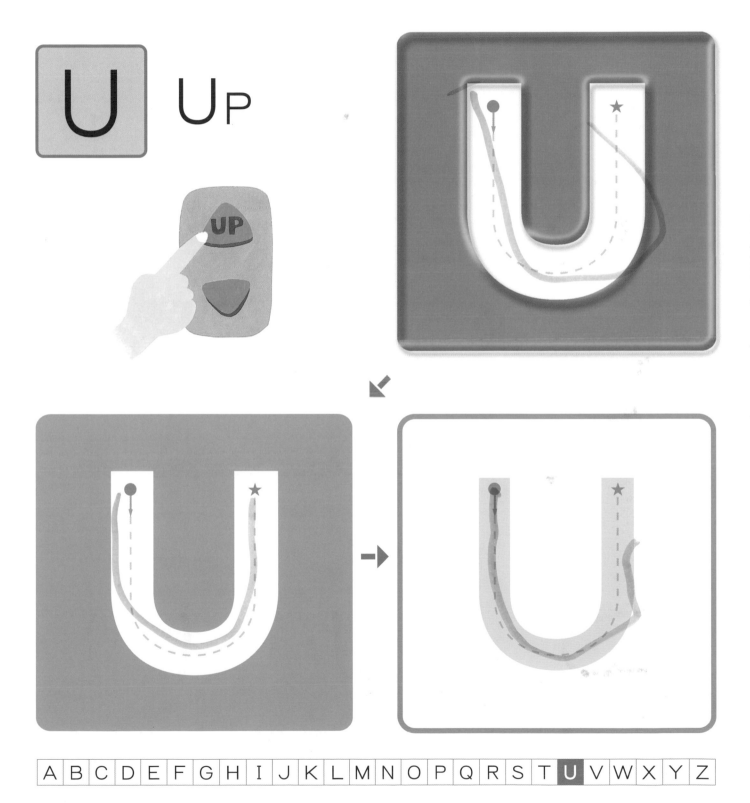

U Up

A B C D E F G H I J K L M N O P Q R S T **U** V W X Y Z

Writing R, J, and U

- Draw a line from the dot (●) to the star (★).
  Follow the order of the numbers.

R_{AT}   J_{AM}   U_P

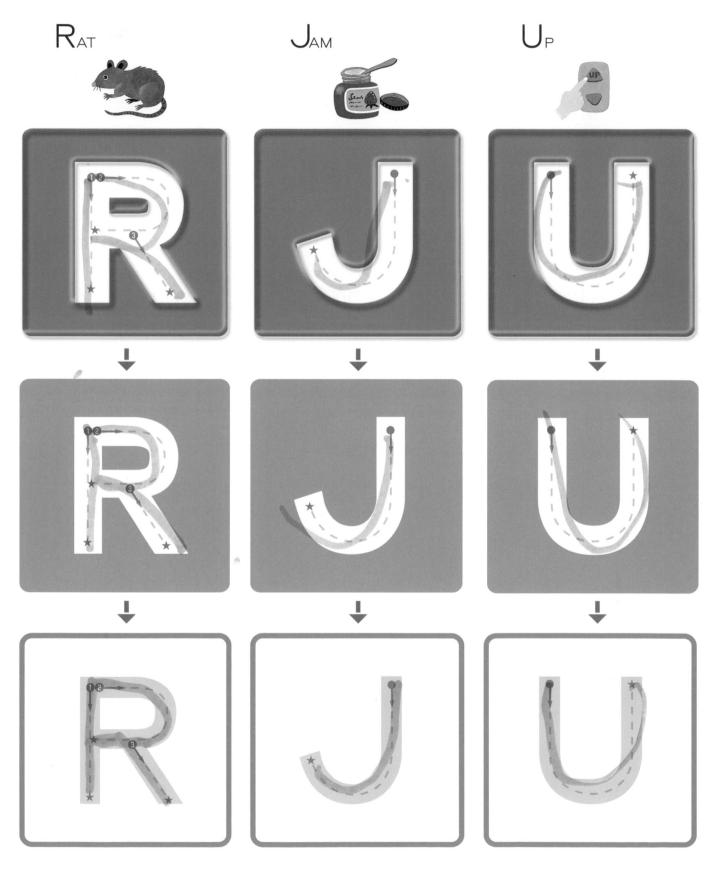

27 Review
Writing D, P, and B

Name

Date

■Draw a line from the dot (●) to the star (★).
  Follow the order of the numbers.

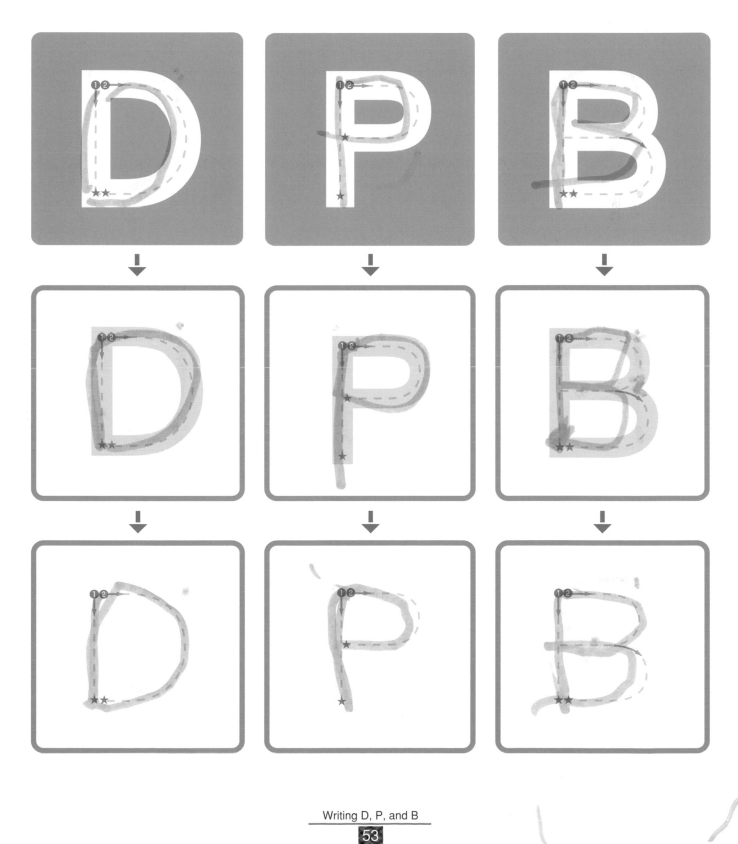

Writing R, J, and U

■Draw a line from the dot (●) to the star (★).
  Follow the order of the numbers.

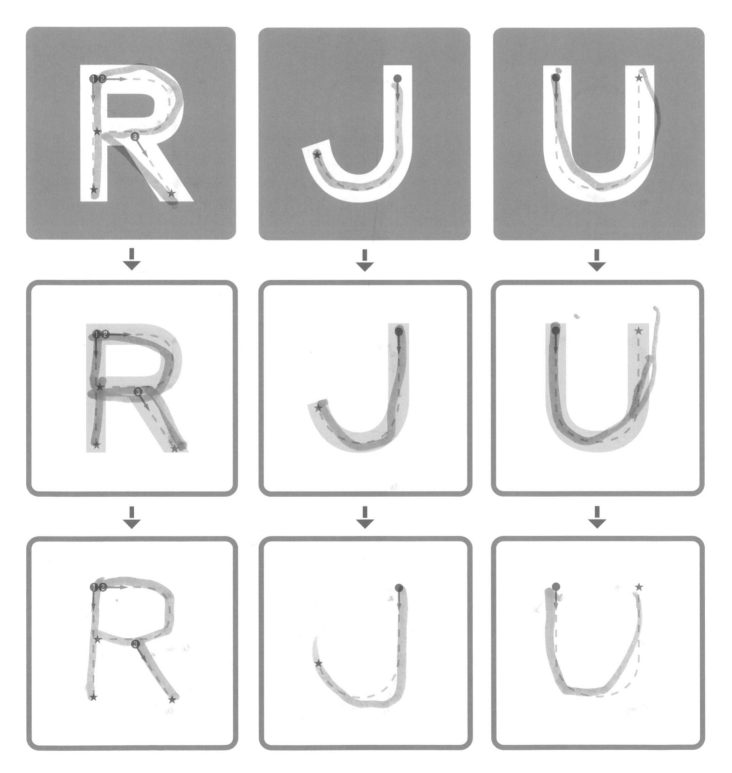

Drawing Wavy Lines

28

Name	
Date	

■Draw a line connecting each pair of pictures.

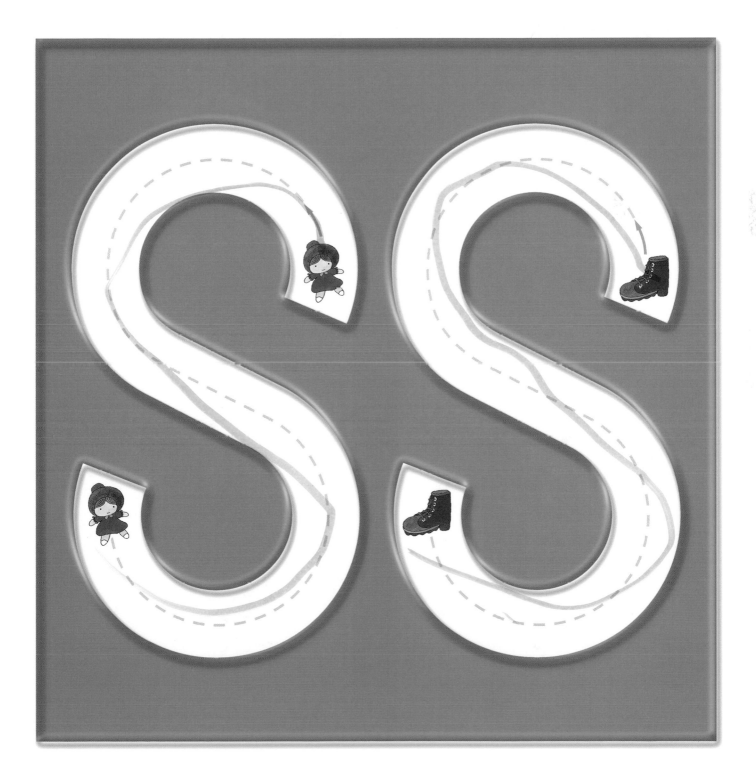

■Draw a line connecting each pair of pictures.

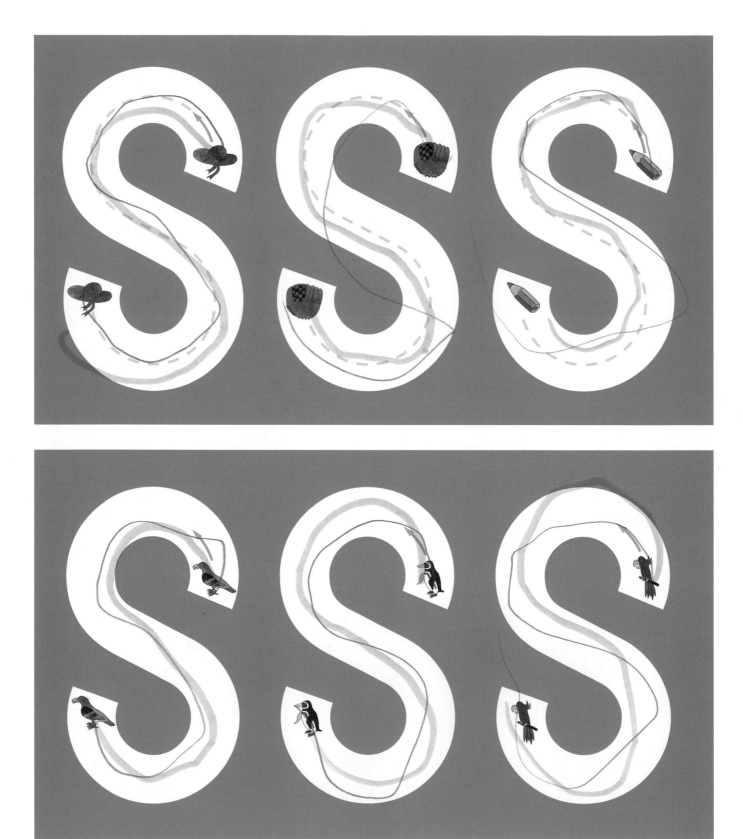

29 Drawing Wavy Lines

Name	
Date	

■Draw a line connecting each pair of pictures.

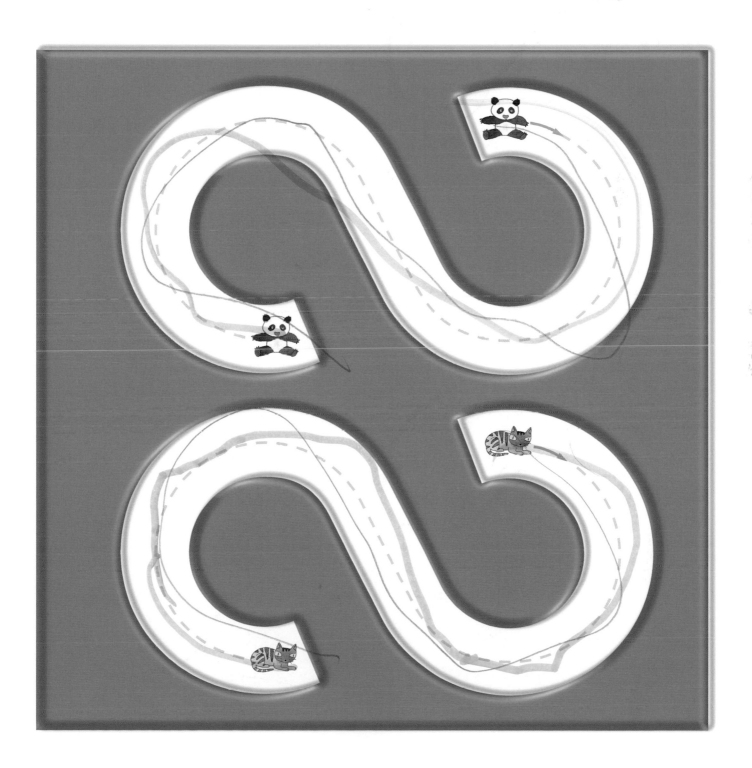

■Draw a line connecting each pair of pictures.

Name

Date

■Draw a line from the dot (●) to the star (★).

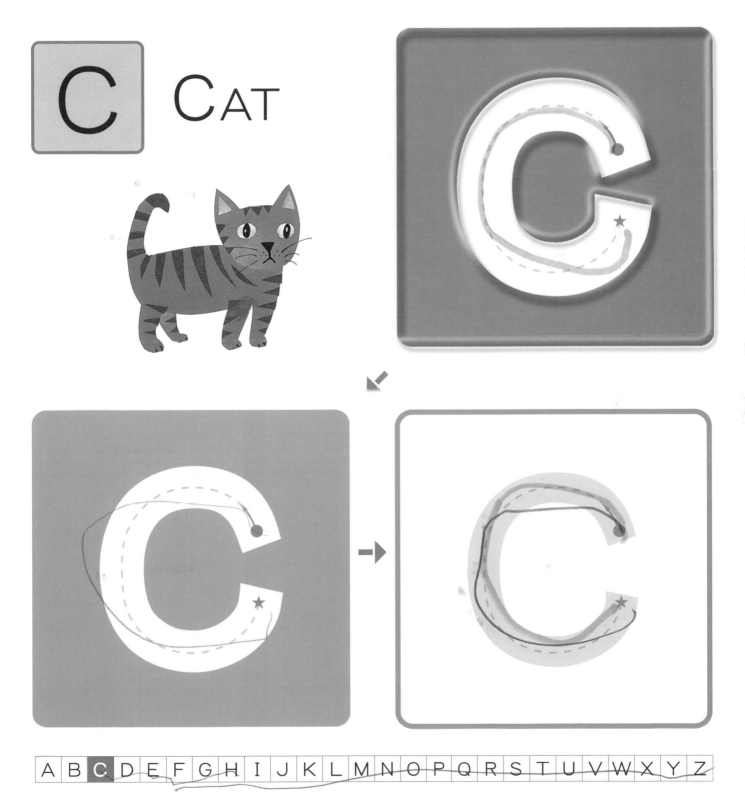

C | CAT

| A | B | C | D | E | F | G | H | I | J | K | L | M | N | O | P | Q | R | S | T | U | V | W | X | Y | Z |

Writing G

Bikes,
Sup
windsurfing

■Draw a line from the dot (●) to the star (★).
Follow the order of the numbers.

G GIFT

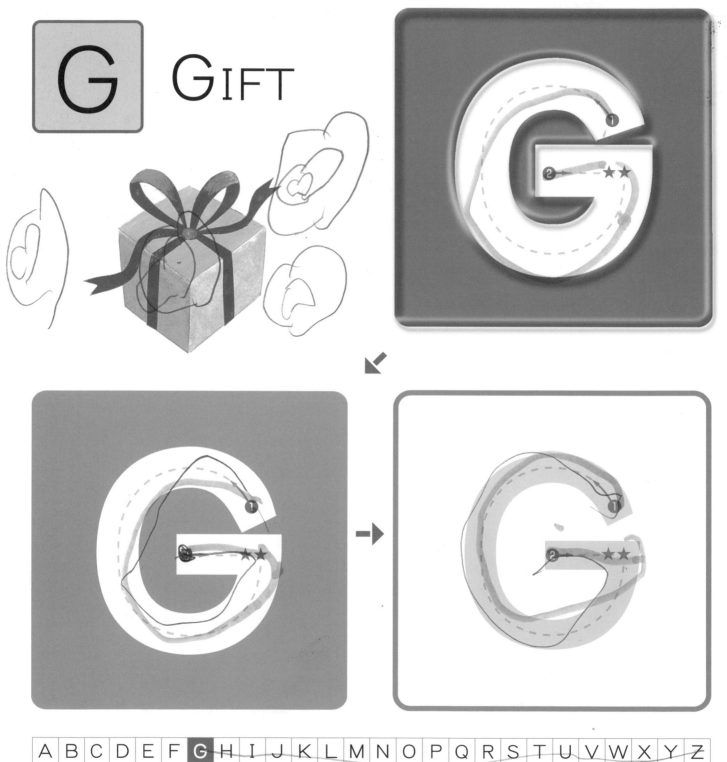

| A | B | C | D | E | F | G | H | I | J | K | L | M | N | O | P | Q | R | S | T | U | V | W | X | Y | Z |

Name	
Date	

■Draw a line from the dot (●) to the star (★).

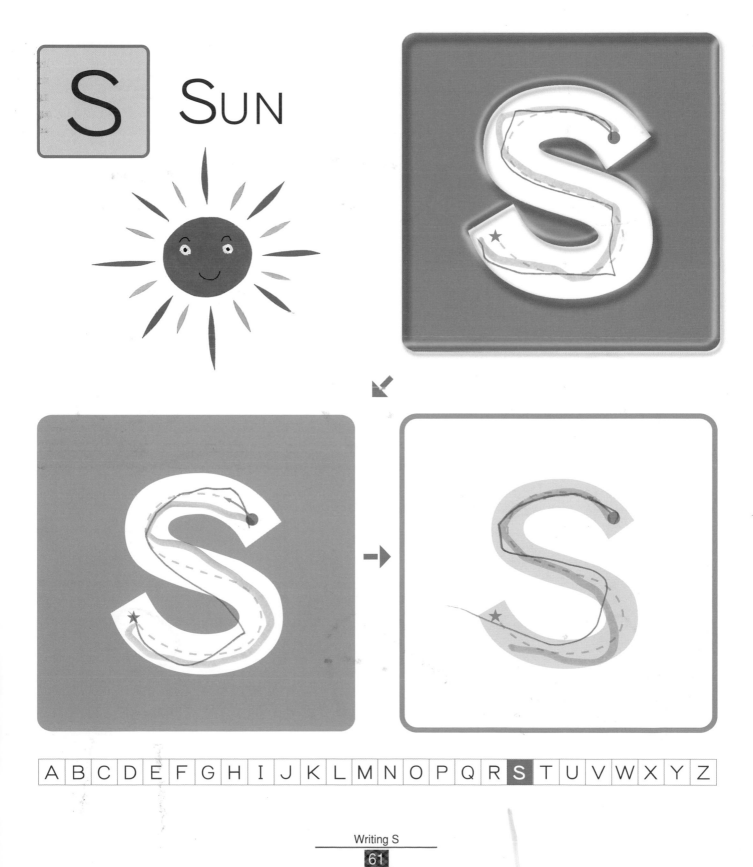

S SUN

A B C D E F G H I J K L M N O P Q R **S** T U V W X Y Z

Writing C, G, and S

▪Draw a line from the dot (●) to the star (★).
Follow the order of the numbers.

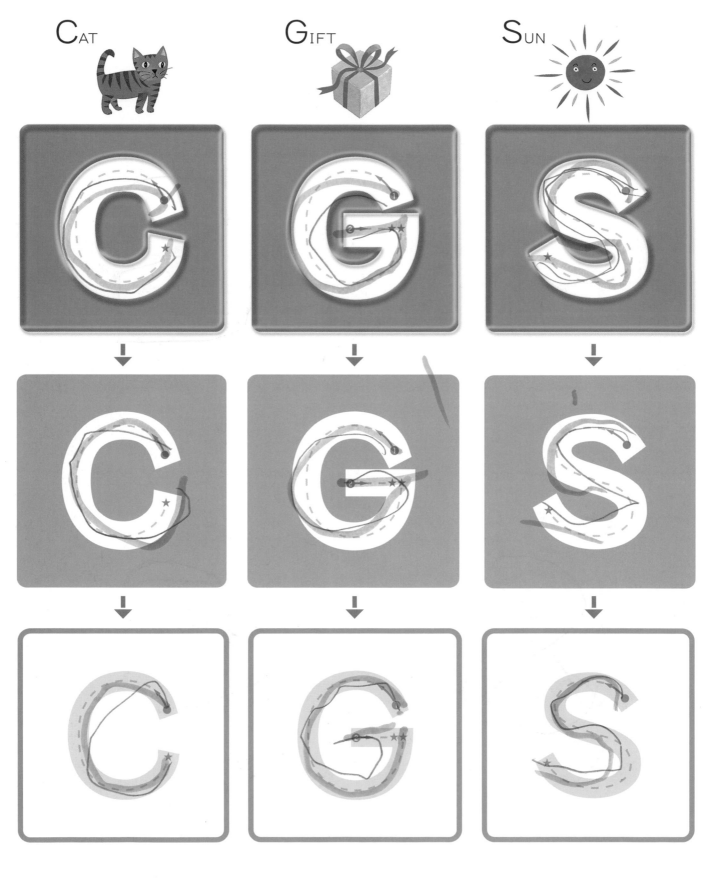

C_{AT}

G_{IFT}

S_{UN}

Drawing Circle Lines

Date

■Draw a line connecting each pair of pictures.

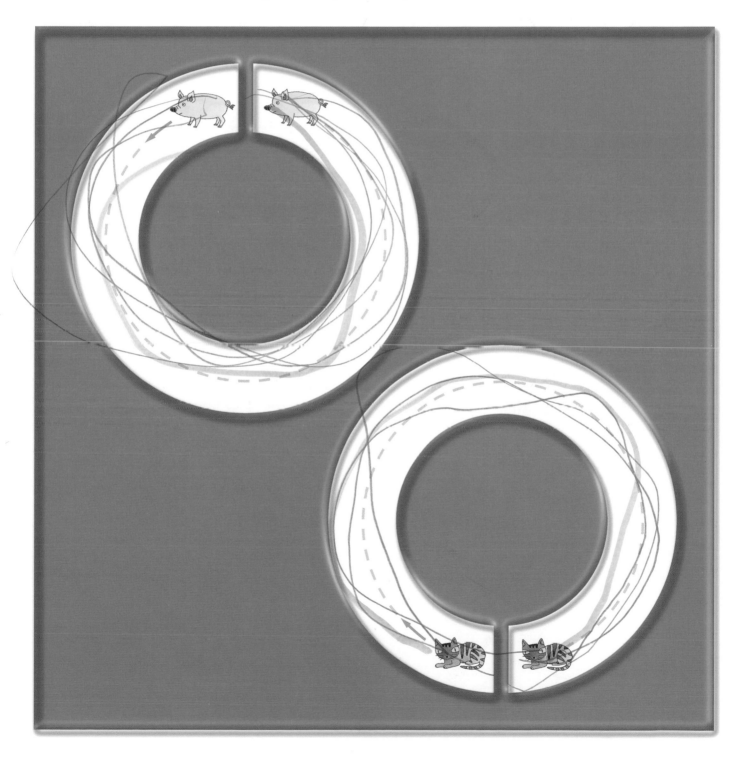

■Draw a line connecting each pair of pictures.

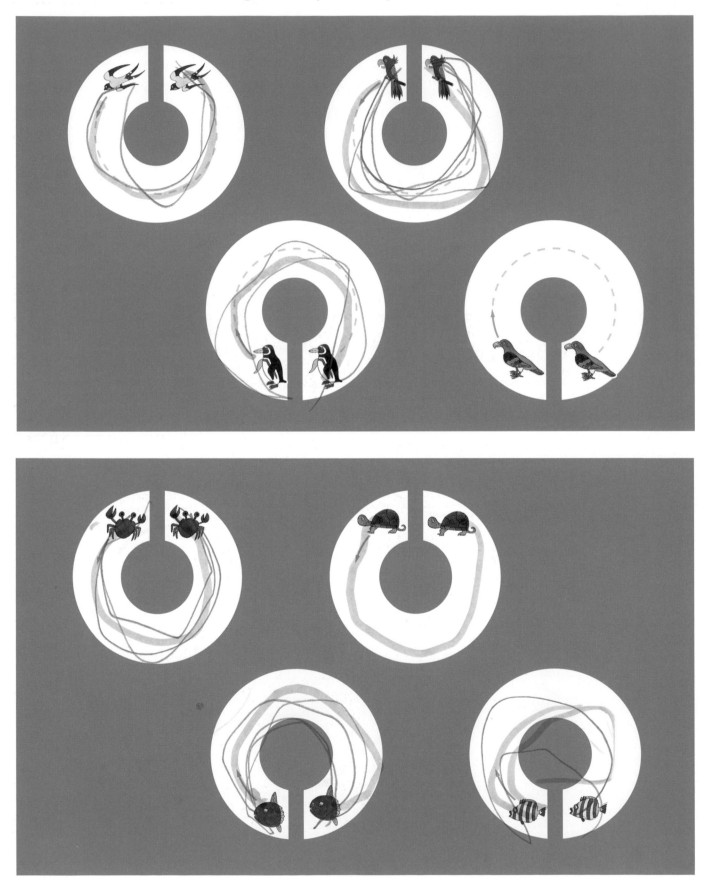

Name	
Date	

■Draw a line from the dot (●) to the star (★).

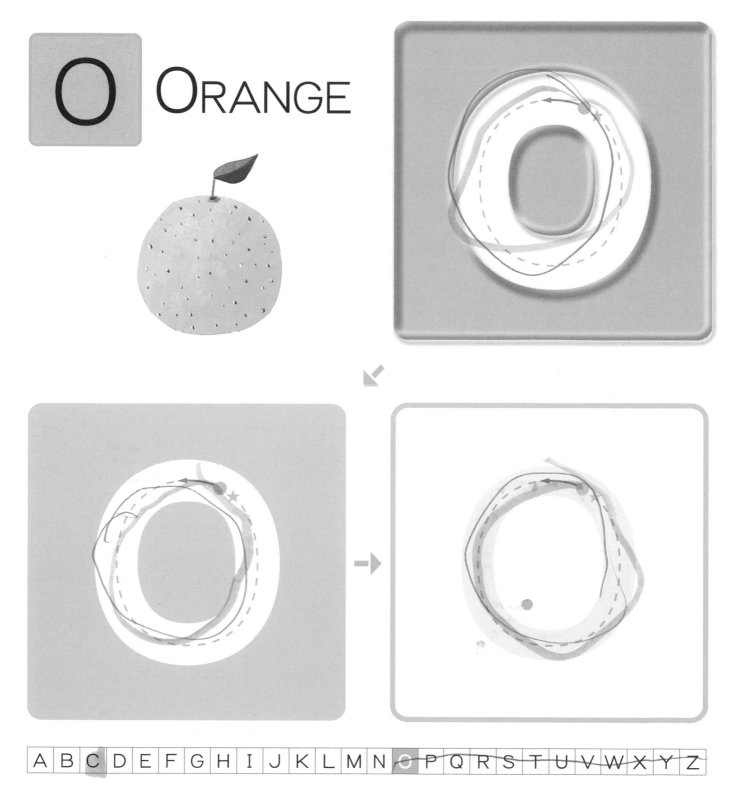

O ORANGE

A B C D E F G H I J K L M N O P Q R S T U V W X Y Z

Writing Q

■Draw a line from the dot (●) to the star (★).
  Follow the order of the numbers.

Q QUEEN

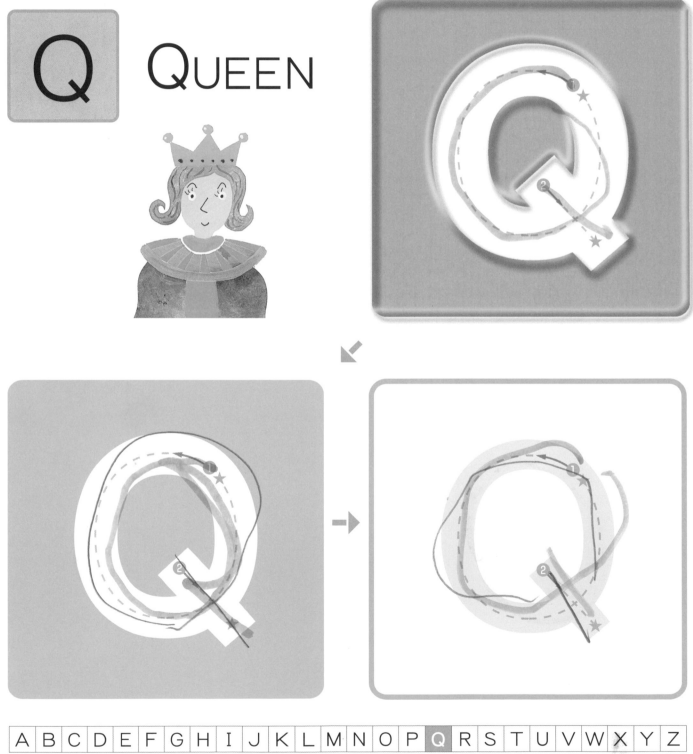

| A | B | C | D | E | F | G | H | I | J | K | L | M | N | O | P | Q | R | S | T | U | V | W | X | Y | Z |

34 Review
Writing C, G, and S

Name

Date

■Draw a line from the dot (●) to the star (★).
 Follow the order of the numbers.

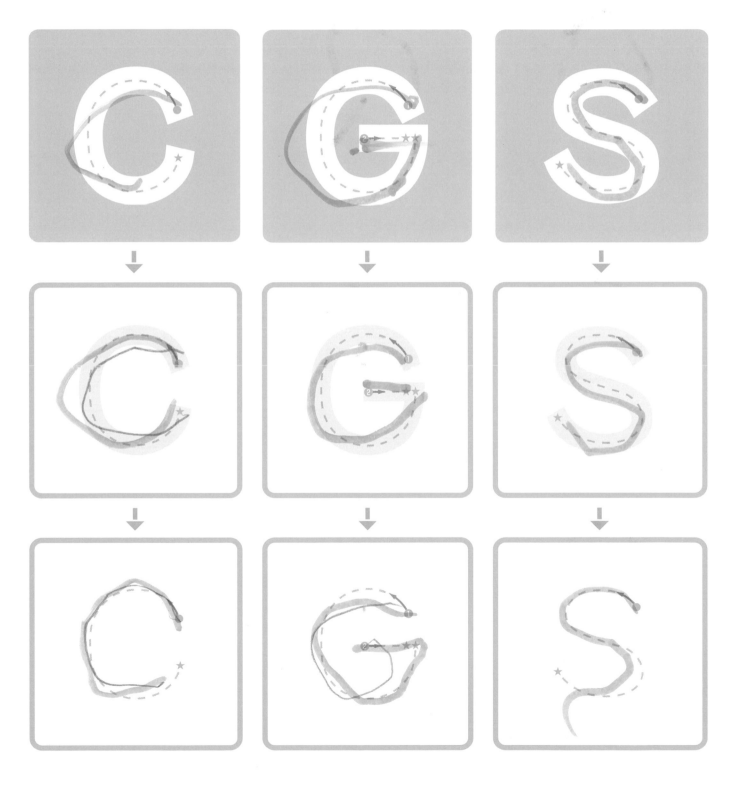

Writing O and Q

■Draw a line from the dot (●) to the star (★).
  Follow the order of the numbers.

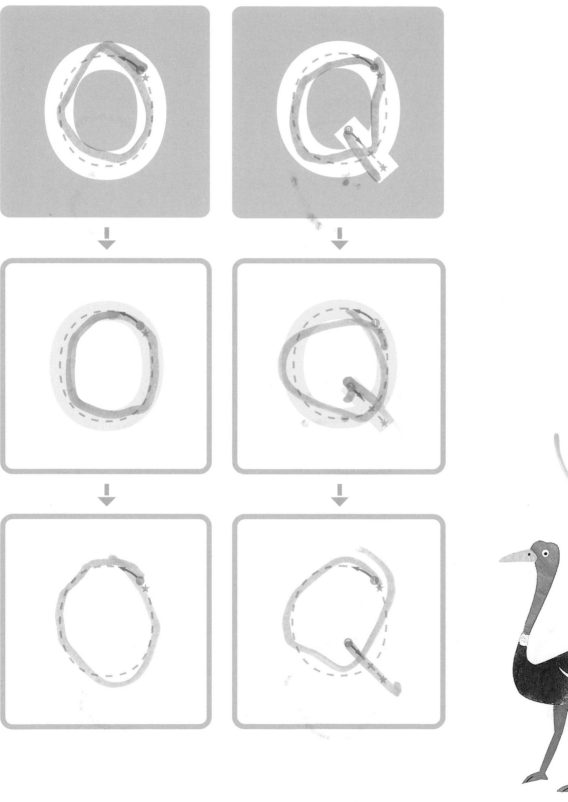

Name

Date

■Trace the letters below.

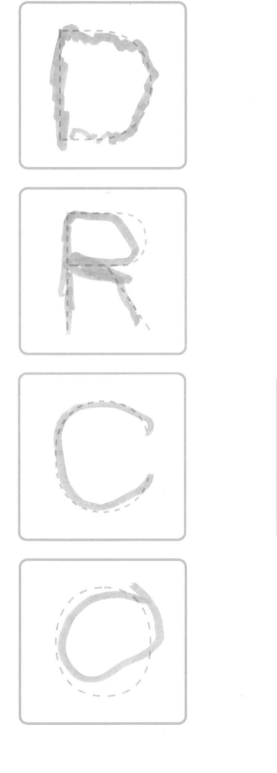

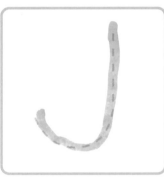

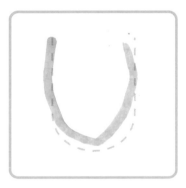

Writing A, B, and C

▪Draw a line from the dot (●) to the star (★).
 Follow the order of the numbers.

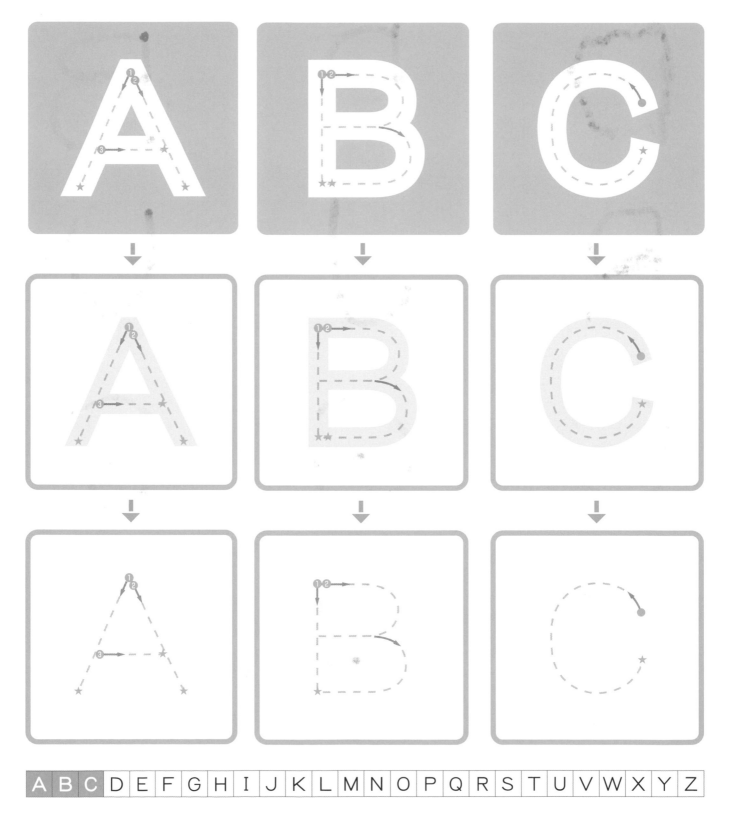

A B C D E F G H I J K L M N O P Q R S T U V W X Y Z

Review

Writing D, E, and F

Name

Date

■Draw a line from the dot (●) to the star (★).
Follow the order of the numbers.

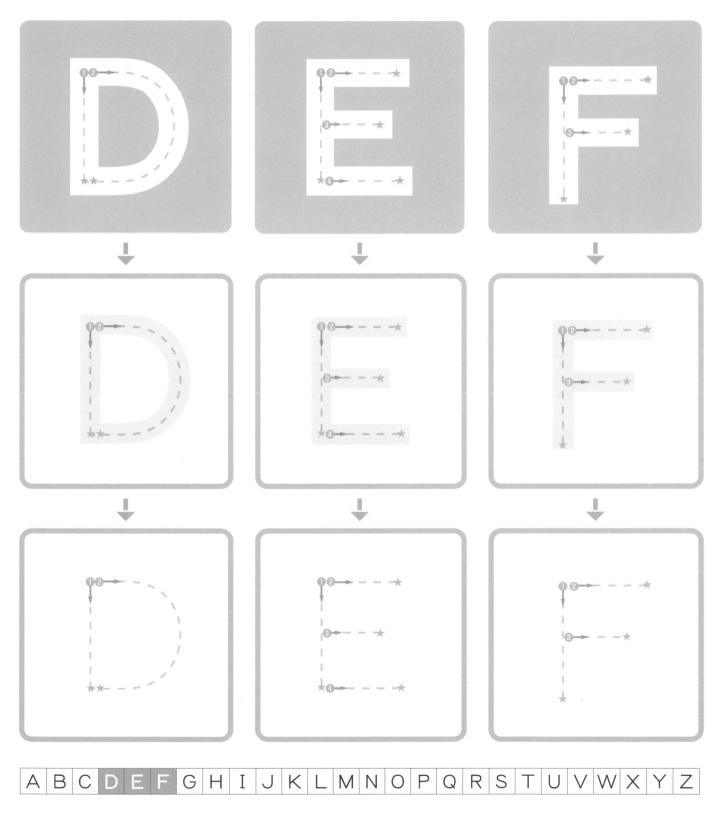

A B C D E F G H I J K L M N O P Q R S T U V W X Y Z

Writing G, H, and I

■Draw a line from the dot (●) to the star (★).
 Follow the order of the numbers.

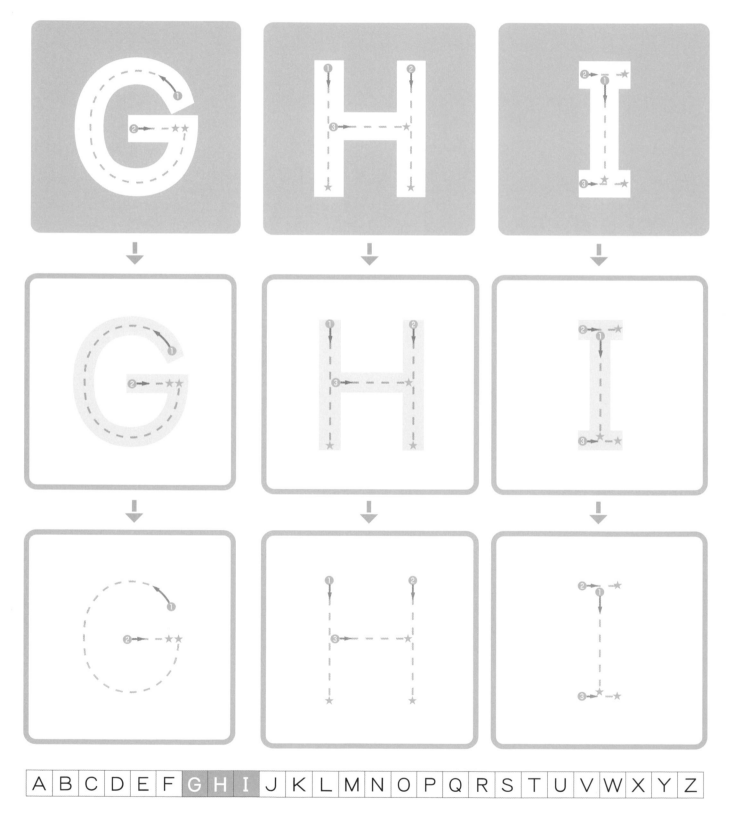

A B C D E F G H I J K L M N O P Q R S T U V W X Y Z

Review
Writing J, K, and L

Name

Date

- Draw a line from the dot (●) to the star (★).
  Follow the order of the numbers.

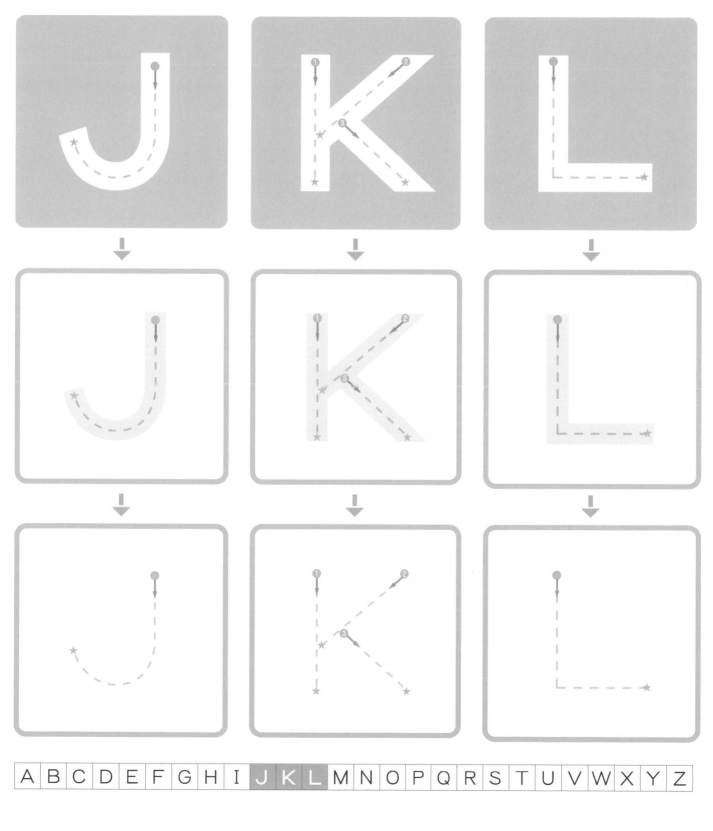

| A | B | C | D | E | F | G | H | I | J | K | L | M | N | O | P | Q | R | S | T | U | V | W | X | Y | Z |

Writing M, N, and O

■Draw a line from the dot (●) to the star (★).
  Follow the order of the numbers.

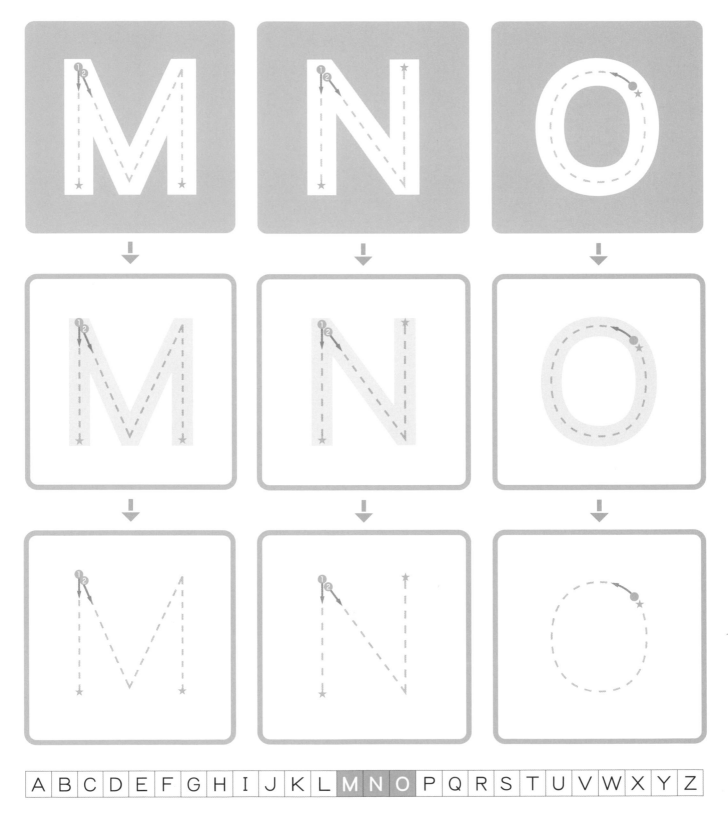

| A | B | C | D | E | F | G | H | I | J | K | L | M | N | O | P | Q | R | S | T | U | V | W | X | Y | Z |

Name

Date

■Draw a line from the dot (●) to the star (★).
Follow the order of the numbers.

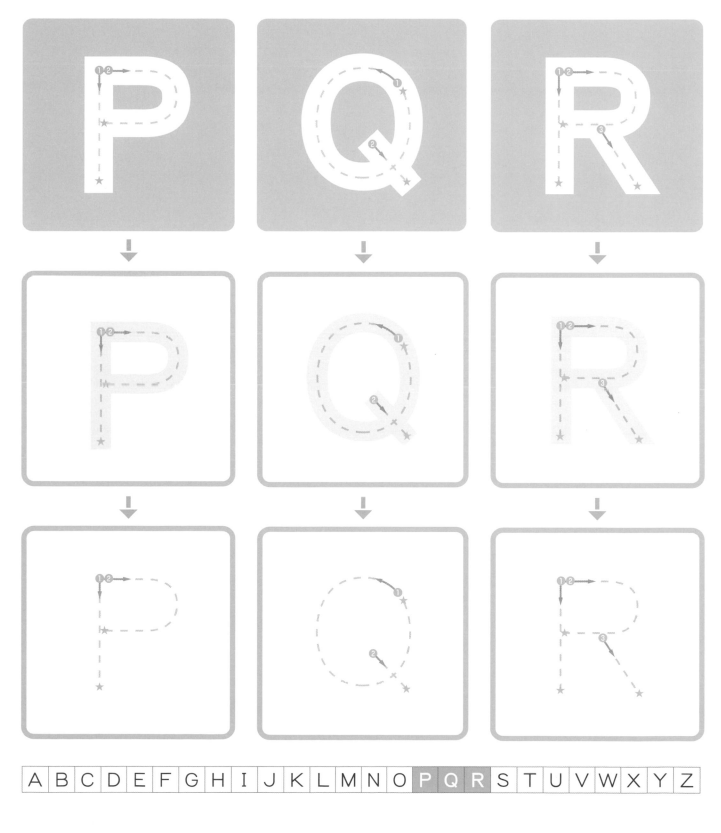

| A | B | C | D | E | F | G | H | I | J | K | L | M | N | O | P | Q | R | S | T | U | V | W | X | Y | Z |

Writing S, T, and U

■Draw a line from the dot (●) to the star (★).
Follow the order of the numbers.

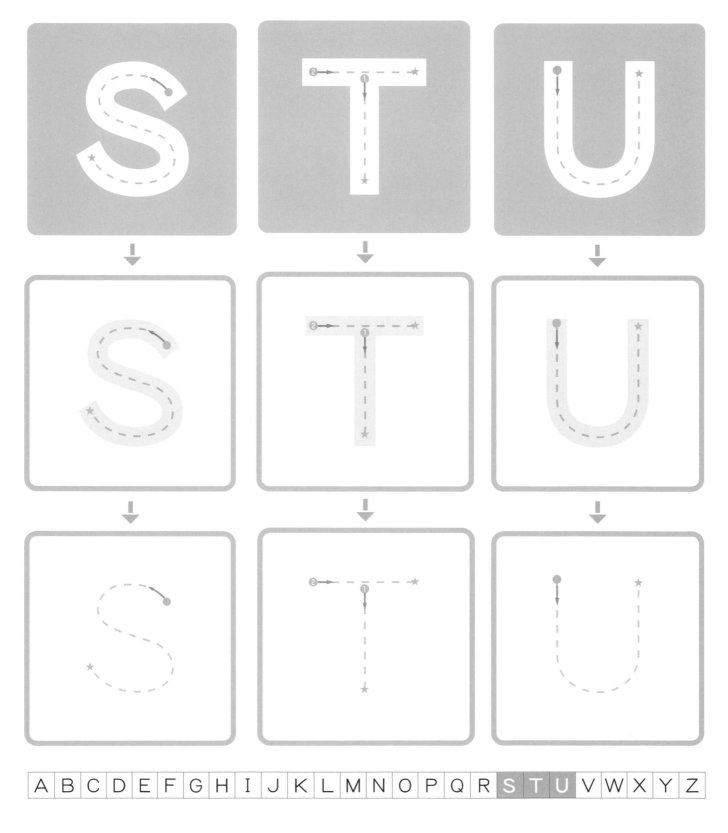

A B C D E F G H I J K L M N O P Q R S T U V W X Y Z

39

Review
Writing V, W, and X

Name

Date

■Draw a line from the dot (●) to the star (★).
Follow the order of the numbers.

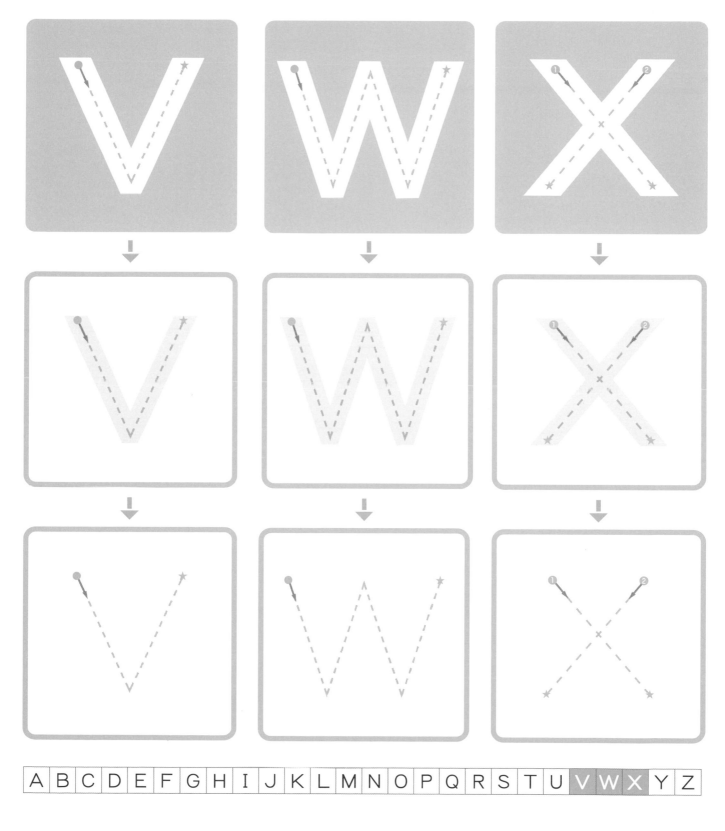

| A | B | C | D | E | F | G | H | I | J | K | L | M | N | O | P | Q | R | S | T | U | V | W | X | Y | Z |

Writing Y and Z

■Draw a line from the dot (●) to the star (★).
Follow the order of the numbers.

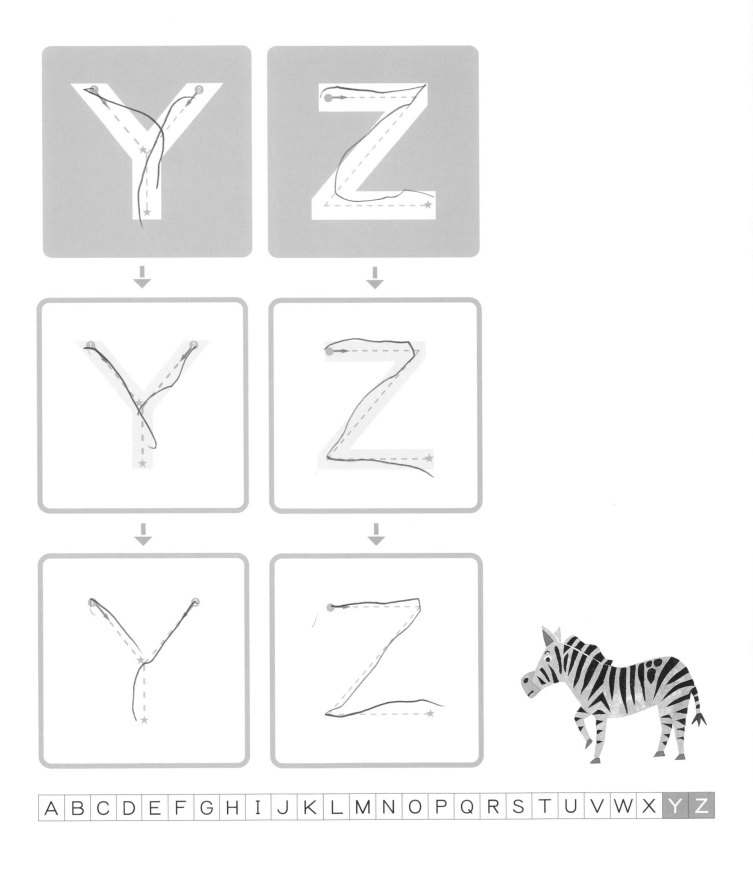

| A | B | C | D | E | F | G | H | I | J | K | L | M | N | O | P | Q | R | S | T | U | V | W | X | Y | Z |

Review
Writing A-Z

Name
Date

■Trace the letters A to Z.

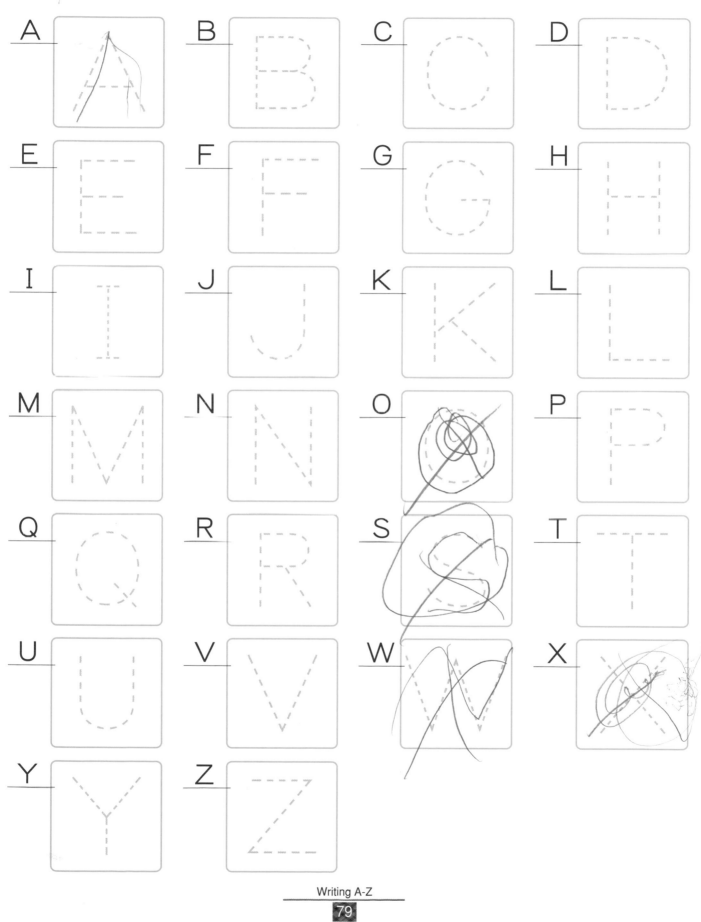

A B C D

E F G H

I J K L

M N O P

Q R S T

U V W X

Y Z

■Write the letters A to Z, as shown on the left.

A ☐ B ☐ C ☐ D ☐

E ☐ F ☐ G ☐ H ☐

I ☐ J ☐ K ☐ L ☐

M ☐ N ☐ O ☐ P ☐

Q ☐ R ☐ S ☐ T ☐

U ☐ V ☐ W ☐ X ☐

Y ☐ Z ☐

You are now able to read and write
uppercase letters A to Z.
Congratulations!

KUMON

Certificate of Achievement

is hereby congratulated on completing

My First Book of Uppercase Letters

Presented on _____ , 20 ____

_____
Parent or Guardian